BEST OF IRISH
FESTIVE COOKING

DELICIOUS MODERN RECIPES

Best of
Irish

BASED ON TRADITIONAL IRISH COOKING

PRAISE FOR THE *BEST OF IRISH* COOKBOOKS:

'This series is fabulous and highly recommended. The books are
packed full of information ... A handy and very neat addition
to any kitchen shelf'

Books Ireland

'Exciting Irish cookbook series.
Easy to follow, zippy and well presented'

Carla Blake, Irish Examiner

'An easy-to-carry gift to bring home as a souvenir of a visit'

RTÉ Guide

'Sound recipes with an Irish flavour ...
And they are quite straightforward'

Georgina Campbell, Irish Independent

BIDDY WHITE LENNON is a founder member and former Chairwoman of the Irish Food Writers Guild. She is the author of several cookbooks, including three previous titles in the *Best of Irish* series: *Potato Recipes, Traditional Cooking* and *Home Baking.* She has written and presented a ten-part television series on healthy eating for the Irish Department of Health.

Biddy writes regularly for *Food and Wine Magazine,* has a cookery column in the *Irish Farmers' Journal* and a column in *Woman's Way* magazine. She gives cookery demonstrations all over Ireland and is a freelance contributor to many publications and a regular broadcaster on television and radio on subjects as varied as health, social welfare, fashion, interiors and travel.

As an actress, she is perhaps best known in Ireland for her portrayal of Maggie in the hugely popular RTÉ television series, *The Riordans,* a role she played for fifteen years. She continued to act in the series when it moved to radio and also co-wrote many episodes with her husband, later writing for the TV series *Glenroe.*

Best of Irish Festive COOKING

BIDDY WHITE LENNON

THE O'BRIEN PRESS
DUBLIN

First published 2005 by The O'Brien Press Ltd,
20 Victoria Road, Dublin 6, Ireland.
Tel: +353 1 4923333; Fax: +353 1 4922777
E-mail: books@obrien.ie
Website: www.obrien.ie

ISBN: 0-86278-930-3

British Library Cataloguing-in-Publication Data
A catalogue record for this title is available from the British Library

1 2 3 4 5 6 7
05 06 07 08 09

Editing, layout, typesetting, design: The O'Brien Press Ltd
Author photograph: Denis Latimer
Internal illustrations: Anne O'Hara
Cover photography: Walter Pfeiffer
Printing: Cox & Wyman Ltd

Contents

Introduction

Féile is the Irish word for a feast or festival, a celebration. The duty of hospitality and a love of feasting and celebration is a deeply ingrained and ancient characteristic of Irish society. If visitors (and sometimes the natives themselves) are today occasionally confused about the origins of our festive days and seasons, they have good reason. They stem not from one culture but from many. Humans arrived in Ireland over nine thousand years ago and since then successive waves of settlers have influenced the calendar customs we observe today.

Each of these peoples brought their own beliefs: the hunter-gatherers who understood the seasonal movements of fish and animals, Neolithic farmers who knew how sun affected the growth of their crops, the Celts who brought with them a whole pantheon of Gods, missionaries from Rome who brought a belief in the One God. The Vikings from Scandinavia, accomplished traders, no doubt enlivened the *óenach* – large scale public assemblies or fairs – where trading of food, livestock, wine and other imported goods was combined with horse racing and athletic games. In later times the Normans, the English and then Scottish planters added to our calendar customs.

The relative importance of some high days and holy days may wax and wane down the millennia but many, rooted in nature as well as culture, are as unchanging as the seasons and some are, quite literally 'writ in stone'.

Newgrange is one of a number of Neolithic tombs near the River Boyne in County Meath. Within a gigantic circular mound is a long passage lined with stone and decorated with abstract art. Certain motifs are favoured at the different tombs: spirals at Newgrange, concentric rectangular motifs at Knowth, rayed circles at Dowth. Newgrange also has a unique structure, a roof box, that allows the rays of the rising sun to shine directly into the back of the chamber for a very few days around the time of the midwinter solstice on 21 December. These huge Boyne Valley tombs predate the Egyptian pyramids. It is reckoned that four thousand people would have been needed to build the Boyne Valley tombs and the structure and design are clearly the work of an advanced, highly organised and stratified society.

But Ireland is littered with Megalithic tombs from even earlier times that show a people with knowledge of the sky and the natural calendar – both essential for agriculture and seafaring.

Another feature of Ireland is a marked reluctance to abandon a custom. With so many cultures influencing contemporary feasts and festivals it can be difficult to disentangle one influence from the other, particularly as the Irish find it possible to believe in several things at once and, to facilitate this, are adept at disguising one thing as another. Throughout this book you'll find evidence that a lingering belief in the 'old gods', coupled with respect for our ancient ancestors and the *foclóir na Síde* (folklore about the mounds in which the spirits of the ancients are supposed to reside) inform many customs during what are, outwardly, Christian feasts and festivals.

It's only a hundred generations since early Christians arrived in Ireland on a mission to instil a belief in Christ and displace the numerous Celtic gods. In some cases they simply transformed the Celtic gods and goddesses into Christian saints; for example, *Imbolc* was the first day of the Celtic year and was associated with Brigit the pagan Earth mother goddess – she was transformed into Saint Brigid, patron saint of cattle and the dairy. Because cattle culture was central to the Celtic way of life, this made St Brigid as important as the Celtic goddess. Sometimes the Christian missionaries (and adoption of new annual calendars) slightly shifted the date of great Celtic festivals: 21 December, the Celts' midwinter celebration of the return of their dead ancestors, was replaced by Christmas on 25 December, a celebration of the birth of Christ. Some, for reasons that are unclear, they left untouched; for instance, *Bealtaine* (the first day of May), one of the four main Celtic festivals that marked the time when cattle would be moved up to summer pastures in the hills. It was never Christianised and remains rich in pagan customs (or superstitions, as the Christian church called them).

The Irish attachment to fairies, which persisted until relatively recent times, especially in rural Ireland, and to traditional practices of appeasement, charms and counter charms, is misunderstood. First of all, the *síoge* (fairies) were not cute little leprechauns but beings from the otherworld who represent the spirit ancestors. At certain times of the year it was believed that the barriers between the natural world and the otherworld were removed and mortals might encounter the fairies as they came out of the burial mounds and ancient dwelling sites to make mischief, like stealing milk, or putting a changeling in the place of a mortal child. If you acknowledge the power of the fairies with rituals that might once have been associated with sacrifices to pagan gods, you acknowledge your pagan ancestors.

Bonfires are an even more direct throwback to ancient rituals. Although the Celtic celebration of Midsummer to mark the summer equinox was merged with the Christian feast of St John, it did not stop the ancient rituals of climbing hills to light fires to the old gods in a form of solar worship and having a rare old time eating, drinking and dancing.

Likewise *Lughnasa*, in August, marked the beginning of the harvest and is associated with the god Lugh, one of the most powerful of the pagan deities. It was a time when great assemblies were held on mountain tops, where fires were lit and offerings of the first fruits of the harvest season were made to the god. The Christian church assigned one such mountain to Ireland's patron saint and even today climbing to the top of Croagh Patrick on 'Reek Sunday' is still a big day for devout Christians. Curiously, Lugh no longer gets much attention; maybe we no longer feel the need to thank the gods for a harvest.

One of the few contemporary feasts with no pagan connections is St Patrick's Day, our national holiday, which is celebrated beyond our shores in many ways more exuberantly than it is in Ireland. The way we mark our national day probably points to the way Irish feasts and festivals may develop in the future. While it is a religious feast day, the celebrations tend more and more towards a secular celebration of being Irish. But, then, there is nothing new in that either.

Ireland is a land of saints. A list in the twelfth century *Book of Leinster* contains 1,100 saints and Irish historian John Ryan has reckoned that in medieval texts listing saints' feast days there are 1,700 named saints. Since Rome began officially canonising saints (as opposed to the earlier method of becoming a saint by acclamation) only four Irish people have actually been canonised. But the medieval period was prime time for sainthood. It was then that the enthusiastic practice of celebrating 'local' saints by 'pattern days' took root. Festivities began with religious devotions, in pre-reformation days in the parish church, and afterwards at the ruin of a church, shrine, or holy well dedicated to the saint. In some locations some of the rituals or traditions are older than Christianity. During penal times the lack of clerical direction allowed greater freedom in the form of devotion and in the secular celebrations that followed. The church tried to keep things under control by banning dancing, musicians and 'other abuses'. The penal laws of the early eighteenth century often legislated against patterns. A particularly infamous act to 'prevent the further growth of Popery and prohibit riotous and unlawful assembling together of many thousands of papists to the said wells and other places' prescribed fines of ten shillings on those who met and twenty shillings on 'vendors of all ale, victuals, or other commodities'.

The arrival of Normans in the twelfth century introduced a different legal system and as a result of agricultural practices brought in a new set of feast days like Michaelmas and Harvest Home which emphasised a shift from cattle to crops. Plantations of settlers from Scotland made New Year's Day a holiday celebrated with some ceremony in the province of Ulster. Also in Ulster, the 12th of July commemorates the victory of King William of Orange over King James II at the Battle of the Boyne. Settlers from England also brought Mothering Sunday, a day when servant girls were allowed to visit home. It's hard to unravel why St Valentine's Day (14 February) only caught the Irish imagination about thirty years ago – given that a pope sent his bones to Dublin in 1836. In a short time it's grown into a commercial success, especially among young lovers.

It is notable that other popular festivals established in the last century – the Oyster Festival in Galway and the Strawberry Festival in Enniscorthy, County Wexford – have no links to pagan gods or to Christianity. What they do have in common is the most ancient reason for celebration: the successful harvesting of food. We have, perhaps, come full circle.

Local festivals abound. In summer time it would be easy to believe there is one round every turn of the road or bend in a river. Some, like the Connemara Pony Fair, or Puck Fair in Killorglin, County Kerry, are linked to older rural customs. Others are connected to the Irish love of performance arts: the *Fleadh Cheoil*, the Dublin Theatre Festival, the Wexford Festival Opera and amateur drama festivals which are held every year in over forty locations in Ireland. There's a Cork Jazz festival, a Cork Film festival, a Dublin Film festival, a Kilkenny Comedy festival and even a Cartoon festival in the village of Rathdrum in County Wicklow. The number of local festivals is matched only by the Summer Schools that celebrate our musical and literary traditions, like the long-established Merriman School and the Sligo Yeats festival. What they all have in common is that they provide the perfect excuse for a feast and some festive spirit to fuel the *craic*. Lest you think the festive spirit is more important than the food, Bloomsday (16 June), which celebrates James Joyce's literary creation Leopold Bloom and his day-long odyssey around the City of Dublin, features food at every turn.

IRISH COFFEE

Probably the best-known Irish whiskey drink in the minds of tourists – but the Irish are pretty fond of it too! Joe Sheridan, who was once the chef at the flying-boat base at Foynes (on the River Shannon but not the town or airport of Shannon), was definitely its creator despite the fact that Shannon Airport claims, and usually gets, the credit. Irish coffees are served in warmed wine goblets.

Ingredients per glass:

1 measure (37.5 ml/2½ tablesp) Irish whiskey

1 measure strong, hot black coffee (enough to come three-quarters way up the glass)

2 teasp sugar

1-2 tablesp fresh double cream, very, very lightly whipped

Method:

Pour the coffee into the glass, add sugar and stir to dissolve. Add whiskey. Position a teaspoon backside up near the rim of the glass and gently pour the cream over the back of the spoon. It should float on the top of the coffee. You cannot make Irish coffee without sugar because it's the sugar in the mixture that allows the cream to float. The liquid is drunk through the cream, which is never stirred in.

Imbolc, 1 February, St Brigid's Day

In Ireland, Spring begins officially on St Brigid's Day, the first day of February, which is also the feast of *Imbolc*, the ancient pagan spring festival and the first day of the Celtic agricultural year. In Irish mythology the father of all the Irish gods was Dagda. He had a daughter, Brigit, designated the mother goddess, the exalted one and goddess of fertility. Her symbol was fire. The fiery dart of Brigit is represented by a sun symbol which, in later times, developed into what we now call St Brigid's cross.

In early Christian times *Imbolc* was taken over and pagan Brigit was transformed into a saint (with a Christian mythology to equal her pagan one). Saint Brigid became Ireland's second patron saint, the patroness of sheep, cattle, dairy work, poets (and much more). Since there are few facts known about the Christian Brigid, there remained a tension between Brigit and the miraculous deeds of St Brigid because so many pagan elements influenced the 'traditional' lore of St Brigid.

The main significance of the feast of St Brigid was that it Christianised one of the pagan focal points of the agricultural year – when preparations for spring sowing were begun and spring lambing started – so St Brigid was given special responsibility for the protection of farm animals and crops. In rural Ireland this feast was a day of stocktaking in household and farmyard: the housewife counted how much meal, bacon, potatoes and other foods she had in store; the farmer considered how long his stock of hay and other winter fodder would last until the grass began to grow again.

The rituals began on St Brigid's Eve. Brigid was supposed to travel about the countryside, accompanied by her favourite white cow, to bestow her blessing on the people and their animals, so a token of welcome was placed on a window sill – a cake or bread and butter for Brigid and a sheaf of corn for her cow.

No matter how poor the household, a festive meal or at least a special dish would be prepared for supper. This varied in different regions but butter always formed part of the meal and was always churned on that day. Some of it might be sent to poor neighbours. 'Strong' farmers killed a sheep and sent meat to the needy, others might send fowl or bacon. Other festive foods included colcannon, dumplings, sowans, apple or ginger cake, curd cake, and fruit cake, or barm brack.

Brigid was a renowned brewer, dispensing copious amounts of ale to all without distinction of rank. Ale was therefore drunk in her memory before the making of the ritual cross from straw or rushes began. A cross was hung in both house and cattle byre as a form of protection and to encourage good luck.

Younger people doing the rounds of local houses to collect food and money for 'a hooley' was a common feature of the festival. A *brideog*, an effigy made from a churn-dash dressed up as a human figure, was carried around the houses by 'biddies' collecting food and money for 'the Biddy'. They usually sang a verse to encourage donations:

Here comes Brigid dressed in white
Give her something for the night.
She is deaf, she is dumb,
She cannot talk without a tongue.

Alas, almost all of these colourful customs have now died out. While a Brigid's cross may still hang near the door of some rural homes, St Brigid gets scant attention. The day is no longer a church holiday and has never been a public holiday. It's now quite rare for a young girl to be named Brigid and the term 'an auld Biddy' is more than a little derogatory and means an interfering, reactionary, gossiping busybody of mature years.

Yet the Brigid of Christian legend is an attractive person, giving clues to the type of woman likely to gain respect in early Christian Ireland: a clever, liberated lady who outwitted chieftains and bishops, wielded a great deal of authority, but was imbued with a Celtic sense of hospitality. She is reputed to have been the best baker of bread and brewer of ale and mead in Ireland and enjoyed a drink as much as the next person.

SPRING TONIC NETTLE SOUP

Nettles are a traditional spring tonic – an ancient Irish way of flushing toxins from the system that actually has some scientific basis. Nettles are rich in iron and also valuable in the treatment of arthritis. Pick only the tender tops (never use tops which have flowered) and use gloves when picking them. It is possible, by harvesting frequently, to keep young nettle tops going right through until the early summer.

SERVES 6

Ingredients:

350 g/12 oz/2 US cups floury potatoes, peeled and cubed

150 g/5 oz/1 US cup mild onion, peeled and finely chopped

3 cups (closely packed) nettle tops, washed and roughly chopped

2 tablesp butter (**or** bacon, duck, or goose fat)

1.5 ltrs/2¹/₃ pts/6 US cups chicken **or** turkey stock

Garnish:

2 tablesp chopped fresh parsley or chives

a little cream, lightly whipped

Method:

Melt the butter in a large pot and sweat the onion and potato for about 10 minutes over a gentle heat. Add the stock and bring to the boil. Wash the nettle tops, drain them and add them to the pot to simmer for 5 minutes only (any longer and the bright green colour fades and a rather strong taste develops). Test for tenderness – don't worry, they don't sting after cooking! Purée the soup until smooth in a foodmill or food processor. Return to the pan and reheat.

Serve garnished with a swirl of cream and the chopped herb of your choice.

Variation:

Before cultivated cabbage was introduced, watercress was the traditional accompaniment to boiled bacon and it still grows wild all over Ireland. It can be used in place of nettles but nowadays you should only buy watercress that has been commercially farmed. Use double the amount of watercress to replace the nettles.

keRRy apple cake

Kerry men (and women and children) are well-known inside and outside Ireland for having jokes told against them. Actually, I've always regarded this as the best Kerry joke of all because, in reality, Kerry people are famous for being 'cute' – clever, on the ball, always keeping the best things secret. In a Kerry apple cake the apples are 'invisible', their presence revealed only when you taste it.

SERVES 4–8

Ingredients:

3 large cooking apples, peeled, cored and diced

225 g/8 oz/2 US cups unsifted white flour

90 g/3 oz butter

90 g/3 oz/(scant) ½ US cup caster sugar

I teasp baking powder

¼ teasp salt

I extra-large egg, beaten

¼ teasp nutmeg, grated (or ground cinnamon or ground cloves)

3 tablesp Demerara sugar

Method:

Grease a 20 cm/8 inch cake tin with butter, then line it with greaseproof paper.

Sift the flour into a bowl and rub in the butter until you have a mixture like fine breadcrumbs. Mix the salt, sugar, and baking powder together in a small bowl, then stir into the flour mixture. Add the chopped apples and the egg and mix to a soft dough. Turn the dough into the cake tin. Mix the Demerara sugar and spice and sprinkle over the top of the cake. Bake at once at 180°C/350°F/Gas 4 for about 45 minutes, or until a skewer inserted into the middle of the cake comes out clean. Traditionally this cake is eaten hot from the oven. It can be served warm (even cold) as long as it is freshly made – just warm it gently if it is to be eaten the following day.

CIÓER CAKE

Apples are a native fruit and cider has been made in Ireland since earliest times. There is still a thriving cider industry and the sight of apple orchards in blossom is uplifting in springtime. Cakes made with apples are traditional on St Brigid's Day.

Ingredients:

110 g/4 oz butter

110 g/4 oz/generous ½ US cup caster sugar

1 teasp bicarbonate of soda

225 g/8 oz/2 US cups unsifted self-raising white flour

½ teasp freshly grated nutmeg

2 medium eggs, beaten

200 ml/7 fl oz/generous ¾ US cup medium sweet cider

2 juicy eating apples, peeled, cored and sliced into wedges (optional)

1–2 tablesp caster sugar for the topping

Method:

Grease a 23 cm/9 inch square, non-stick baking tin with butter. Cream the butter and sugar until light and fluffy. Sift the flour, nutmeg and bicarbonate of soda together. Beat a tablespoon of the flour mix into the butter and sugar mixture followed by all the eggs. Mix in half the remaining flour. Add the cider and beat in fully. Mix in the rest of the flour. Pour the mixture into the tin. If using the apples insert the slices into the mixture (wide side facing upwards) in an even pattern. Bake immediately at 180°C/350°F/Gas 4 for 35–45 minutes or until the top is golden, the cake begins to shrink from the sides of the tin, and the top feels springy to the touch. Allow to cool slightly in the tin before turning out carefully. Place right side up and sprinkle the top with caster sugar. This cake is also lovely eaten as a dessert while still warm served with whipped cream.

Variation:

Replace the apple with peeled, sliced wedges of dessert pear.

Sᴛ Valenᴛine's Day

Mystery surrounds St Valentine. There is confusion even about which of three saints and martyrs bearing the name actually came to be regarded as the patron saint of lovers. According to legend, the favourite is the one who hailed from Rome and was martyred because he resisted an edict of the Roman Emperor Claudius II forbidding the marriage of young men bound for military service – for which offence this Valentine was put to death in AD269 or 270. The date chosen for Valentine's feast day may be connected with the fact that mid-February was when the pagan festival of Lupercal was celebrated (when Roman men and girls chose one another as partners). Another possible link is the belief that birds paired on 14 February, a legend that inspired Geoffrey Chaucer's *Parliament of Fowls*.

A fact little known outside Ireland is that the Carmelite friars of Whitefriar Street Church in Dublin claim to have the remains of the body of this Roman Valentine. What is more, they have a letter to prove provenance. In 1835, Fr John Spratt so impressed Pope Gregory XVI with his powers as a preacher that the pope decided to make a gift of St Valentine's body to Spratt's church in Dublin. The letter which accompanied the body when it arrived in Dublin in 1836 states that the remains are a gift 'freely given to the Very Reverend Father Spratt, Master of Sacred Theology of the order of Calced Carmelites of the convent of that order in Dublin in Ireland, the blessed body of St Valentine, martyr, which we ourselves by the command of the most Holy Father Pope Gregory XVI on the 27th day of December 1835 have taken out of the cemetery of St Hippolytus'.

The exchange of tokens of affection between lovers really only caught on in the nineteenth century. It became popular in Ireland only in the past few decades, but now it's celebrated here enthusiastically by lovers of all ages.

The two foods most commonly associated with Valentine's Day are oysters and chocolate; oysters because of their (almost mythical) aphrodisiac qualities and chocolate because hand-made Irish chocolates are now considered a gift luxurious enough to bestow on your love.

It's very much a day for taking the object of your desire out to dine. Most restaurants are booked out weeks in advance and most put on special dinners many of which feature oysters and chocolate on the menu.

Native Irish oysters are in season from September to April (when there is an 'r' in the name of the month). Pacific Oysters are now cultivated all around our coast and are harvested all year round. The Irish have eaten oysters enthusiastically since the first hunter-gatherers arrived on the island nine thousand years ago; vast mounds of oyster shells have been uncovered in their kitchen middens in estuaries where oysters were plentiful.

OYSTERS, IRISh-STYLE

1 dozen oysters per person is a generous portion – many are satisfied with a half dozen.

Oysters must be tightly shut. Any shell that is even slightly open should be thrown away. To prise them open, place them on a work surface with the round side of the shell facing down. Wrap your left hand in a cloth. Place the oyster in your left palm, flat side uppermost. Push the point of the short, blunt oyster knife into the hinge. Press the middle fingers of your left hand on to the shell. Wiggle the knife blade to left and right then (carefully) jerk up the knife to prise the shells apart. Free the oyster from its root base and turn it best side up, taking care all the while not to lose any of the delicious juice.

True oyster-lovers spurn any additions and eat them straight from the shell, washed down by the juices lingering there. Sometimes a plate of sliced brown 'cake' (soda bread) and butter is served, but only to mop up the traditional pint of stout that inevitably, and gloriously, accompanies the public devouring of oysters. There's even a very good micro-brewery in Dublin that flavours one of its stouts with oysters!

Chocolate Almond Tart

Celtic Irish Chocolate is one of the few Irish companies producing culinary chocolate, and very good it is too. It was a recent winner of the Irish Food Writers Guild Chocolate Lovers Award.

Ingredients:

3 large eggs, beaten

110 g/4 oz Celtic fine dark chocolate

60 g/2 oz /4 level US tablesp butter

200 ml/7 fl oz golden syrup

150 g/5 oz sugar

1 teasp vanilla essence

a few drops almond essence

225 g/8 oz sliced almonds, toasted

one 23 cm (9 inch) sweet shortcrust pastry case, unbaked

Garnish:

a little whipped cream, a purée of red berries or a few redcurrants

Method:

In a bowl set over hot (but not boiling) water melt the chocolate and butter. Warm the golden syrup slightly and whisk it together with the sugar, eggs, vanilla and almond essence. Combine with the melted chocolate and butter and finally, gently stir in the sliced almonds. Pour this filling into the pastry case. Bake at 180°C/350°F/Gas 4 for about 50 minutes, or until the filling is set around the edges but still slightly soft and tender in the middle. Should the pastry brown too quickly cover the tart loosely with foil.

Cool before serving. Serve with whipped cream on top, or with a purée of berries, or some redcurrants on the side.

Shrovetide and Lent

The three days that precede the beginning of Lent were known as Shrovetide, a time of last-minute celebrations before the austerity of the 'black' Lenten fast. It was a popular time for weddings (which were banned during Lent) and wherever there was a wedding there was a feast – one in which all the neighbours joined. Now, in a more secular Ireland, Shrove Tuesday is called Pancake Tuesday.

For hundreds of years, Roman Catholics were bound by church law to abstain from eating meat, eggs, milk (either sweet or sour), butter, cheese, curds and white meats during the forty days of the Lenten fast. This was a severe restriction on people whose main diet consisted of milk products. No animal fats could be used in cooking; bread, which was risen with buttermilk and soda, was also forbidden. The pot and the pan used to cook meat was put away. There was no merrymaking, no dancing or card games; even the rambling houses, where people gathered to make music and tell stories, fell quiet. Families who could afford it laid in a supply of salted, or pickled herrings; even the poor would hope to have a few red herrings hanging from the rafters alongside the salted ling.

Herrings were grilled on a gridiron or just held before the fire using tongs. Ling was boiled in a skillet. Small amounts of these preserved fish were used as a savour to flavour potatoes, or eaten with unleavened oat cakes. Those who lived near the sea gathered edible seaweeds like dillisk (dulse), or carrageen, and shellfish. 'Bull's milk' made by soaking oatmeal husks, was used to colour tea.

A lucky few might get a taste of the barnacle goose. It was common belief from medieval times that this goose did not constitute meat. Gerald of Wales in his *History and Topography of Ireland* (written in the early part of the twelfth century) believed that the goose was hatched from shellfish. Others from this period maintained that it was hatched from a worm, or grew from waterlogged driftwood – a convenient notion that applied to fishy-tasting puffins as well as the barnacle goose. The Culdee monks at Tallaght near Dublin went one better. In the eighth century they decided that it was permitted to eat all wild swine, deer, or fowl.

The ordinary people, however, did observe the black fast of Lent, apart from a short period in the middle of the nineteenth century during the worst of the famine years, when those whose meals were 'scanty or uncertain' were told they should eat whatever they could get. Small wonder that Shrove Tuesday was celebrated with such wistful pleasure.

The feast was a last fling, a home-based celebration with family and friends. All the fresh eggs, milk and butter left in the house were used to make pancakes. These were cooked over a fire that was (in some areas) fuelled by the remains of the Christmas holly branches. Tossing the pancake was the task of the unmarried boys and girls, and their success, or otherwise, in tossing It perfectly so that it landed back on the surface of the pan without a ruffle or crease was said to foretell their marriage fortunes for the year ahead.

BUTTERMILK PANCAKES

MAKES 10–15 depending on size

Method:

Ingredients:

600 ml/20 fl oz/2¼ US cups buttermilk (or sour milk)

150 g/5 oz fine oatmeal

75 g/3 oz self-raising flour

2 tablesp honey

1 teasp baking soda (bicarbonate of soda)

1 egg

enough milk to mix a batter

In a bowl add the oatmeal to the buttermilk; mix well and leave to soak overnight. The next day, sift together the flour and the baking soda and mix them into the oatmeal batter. Add the honey, the beaten egg and just enough milk to make a batter which is slightly thinner than for ordinary pancakes.

Grease a heavy pan or griddle lightly with butter; heat over a medium heat and, when it is hot, place tablespoonfuls of the batter on it. Leave them until they rise and are covered in bubbles and little holes on top. Turn over to brown on the other side (this will not take as long). Best eaten hot from the pan with butter and honey, or with honey and whipped cream.

pancakes

MAKES 10–12

Ingredients:

2 eggs, beaten

110 g/4 oz plain flour

125 ml/4 fl oz/½ US cup milk

125 ml/4 fl oz/½ US cup water

15 ml/1 tablesp melted butter

Method

Put the flour into a bowl, make a well in the centre and put in the beaten eggs. Whisk the eggs and flour until you have a thick paste. Mix the milk and water and slowly whisk into the egg and flour paste. You should end up with a batter which has the consistency of thin cream. Allow to stand for a little while.

Heat a frying pan until it is quite hot. Grease it with a little of the melted butter (use folded kitchen paper dipped in the butter to wipe the pan). Pour about two tablespoons of the batter onto the hot pan. then tilt it rapidly so that the batter spreads evenly over the base. Cook over a medium heat until the pancake surface has bubbles and little holes all over. Turn with a palette knife and cook the other side for slightly less time. Serve and eat each pancake, sprinkled with sugar and lemon juice, before cooking the next one.

Cooked pancakes will keep for two or three days in the fridge and can be reheated, with either a savoury or a sweet stuffing and a sauce.

Suggestions:

Spread 1–2 tablespoons of cooked puréed apple along the centre of each pancake, then roll it up. Pour a few tablespoons of apple juice into a well-buttered rectangular baking dish. Arrange the pancake rolls in one layer in the dish and reheat in an oven set to 180°C/350°F/Gas 4 until hot through. Alternatively, try sliced fresh strawberries warmed in orange juice.

A savoury filling, such as creamy fish pie, can be reheated in a little cream.

Little potato pancakes

A cross between a pancake and a potato cake, these tasty morsels are good on their own, or as a vegetable side dish, or to accompany the traditional 'Full Irish Breakfast'.

MAKES 20

Ingredients:

4 large floury potatoes, cooked and mashed while hot

2 eggs

3 tablesp plain white flour

1 teasp baking powder

200 ml/7 fl oz/¾ US cup of milk

Salt and freshly ground black pepper

Method:

Whisk together the eggs, flour, baking powder and about half the milk. Quickly stir in the mashed potatoes and mix really well. Add enough milk to make a thick batter. Season with salt and freshly ground black pepper.

Choose a wide non-stick pan or griddle; heat it and grease lightly. Drop as many tablespoonfuls of the batter as you can fit onto the hot griddle. Cook for about 3 minutes or until bubbles rise to the surface and the underside is well browned. Turn over with a palette knife and brown the other side. Keep hot while you cook the rest of the batter.

Variations:

Add chopped scallions, crisply cooked and finely chopped bacon rashers, or cooked and finely chopped mushrooms.

the Full Irish

Mothering Sunday

Mothering Sunday was celebrated on the fourth Sunday of Lent and was a day when people travelled to visit the mother church of their parish, and children working as servants or apprentices were allowed home to visit their parents. It was not a native Irish tradition but travelled across the Irish Sea; by the sixteenth century, it had become the practice for maidservants working in Anglo-Norman households within 'the Pale' (the sphere of Norman influence in Ireland) to bake a cake to bring home to their mother on that day.

Originally this cake was simply a spiced fruit bread but in the late nineteenth century it developed into a rich plum cake with a layer of almond paste in the centre. Because the Lenten fast prohibited eating the cake, it was kept until Lent was over and so the cake gradually became associated with Easter and evolved into the Simnel cake as we now know it – a rich fruit cake decorated with eleven or twelve balls of marzipan placed around the rim, symbolising the twelve apostles of Christ.

If the maidservant was unable to bake her cake – perhaps because her employers failed to supply the costly ingredients in the traditional manner, or she had failed to acquire the skills she'd been sent to learn in the big house – her young man might get one baked and present it to her with the verse:

> *And I'll to thee a simnel bring*
> *For when thou goes a-mothering;*
> *So when thy mother blesses thee*
> *Half the blessing thou'll give to me.*

The old traditional Mothering Sunday has been overshadowed by the unrelated North American custom of Mother's Day and is mainly marked by the family going to a special Mother's Day luncheon at a local restaurant. Instead of the elegant Simnel cake, gaudy iced concoctions carrying the message 'Happy Mother's Day' are on offer in cake shops.

SIMNEL CAKE

The small balls of almond paste on this cake represent the apostles of Jesus. Some people make all twelve, but others omit Judas (on the basis that he betrayed Jesus) and only place eleven balls around the edge of the cake.

Ingredients:

110 g/4 oz butter

110 g/4 oz soft brown sugar

3 large eggs, beaten

150 g/5 oz plain white flour

¼ teasp salt

½ teasp cinnamon, ground

½ teasp nutmeg, ground

350 g/12 oz mixed dried fruits (sultanas, currants and raisins)

60 g/2 oz mixed (candied) peel

zest of half a lemon

a little apricot jam

For the almond paste:

175 g/6 oz almonds, ground

175 g/6 oz caster sugar

2 small (or one very large) egg, beaten

½ teasp almond essence

Method:

Preheat oven to 140°C/275°F/Gas 1. Make the almond paste: mix together the sugar and almonds and add just enough egg to give a soft consistency. Knead until the paste is smooth and pliable. Take one third of the paste and roll into a circle 18cm/7inches in diameter. Repeat with another third of the mixture. From the remaining paste form eleven or twelve balls.

To make the cake, cream the butter and sugar together until fluffy. Beat the eggs into the mixture a little at a time. Sift the flour, salt and spices together, then fold into the mixture. Fold in the fruits and lemon rind, mixing well.

Place half the mixture in an 18cm/7 inch deep cake tin (greased and lined with baking parchment). Smooth the top and place a layer of almond paste over it. Add the remaining mixture and smooth the top, hollowing the centre slightly. Bake for 1¾–2 hours, or until a skewer inserted into the cake comes out clean. Don't let the skewer reach the layer of almond paste or you'll get a false result! Take the cake out of the oven and cool for about 30 minutes. Spread the jam on top and lay the second layer of paste over this. Dampen the balls of paste slightly and set around the edge of the cake. Brown very lightly in a 180°C/350°F/Gas 4 for 8–10 mins.

St Patrick's Day, 17 March

St Patrick came to Ireland to preach the faith to Irish pagans living 'at the ends of the earth'. Some historians maintain that there were (at least) two St Patricks and that other Christian missionaries came here before him, but the fact that his influence was (probably) mainly in the northern half of the island is widely acknowledged, but considered unimportant. He is our patron saint and, what is more, we chose him long before formal canonisation was introduced by Rome. Patrick died sometime between AD463 and 493.

By the eighth century, 17 March had been designated as the feast of St Patrick's 'falling asleep'. A hundred years later a note in the *Book of Armagh* directed all churches and monasteries to honour his memory by celebrating for three days and nights in mid-spring. The feast has long been known simply as Patrick's Day and, affectionately, as Paddy's Day. In towns and villages throughout the country parades celebrate culture and commerce equally and flow into other events like dances, concerts and race meetings. In Dublin the three-day festival has taken on an even more secular note, complete with a national parade that features marching bands and drum majorettes from all over the world, street entertainments, firework displays over the River Liffey and free pop concerts in Merrion Square.

The international practice of celebrating Patrick's Day appears to have begun among the Irish diaspora in Europe in the eighteenth century and spread from there to America and the rest of the New World. In days gone by there was good reason for this celebration. Traditionally, the day was one for feasting but 17 March always falls during Lent, a time of severe fasts when the eating of meat was forbidden. In honour of St Patrick, the fast was set aside for that one day and everyone could have meat.

The explanation why the meat eaten on the feast day used to be called 'St Patrick's fish' is given in a *Life of St Patrick* written by a monk called Jocelin in the twelfth century. Patrick, when a young monk, was tempted to eat meat during Lent and hid a piece of pork to eat in secret. However, before he ate it he repented his sin so sincerely that God sent an angel to comfort him. The sight of the angel stunned Patrick into swearing off meat for life and he asked God to send him a sign that he was truly pardoned. Bidden by the angel to plunge the hidden meat into water and take it out again, he did so and, to his astonishment, saw that the meat had been transformed into fish. Patrick used this story to teach his disciples the need to control their appetites. As Jocelin records, the plain people of twelfth-century Ireland gave it a slant that he hardly intended: 'Many of the Irish wrongfully misunderstanding this miracle are wont on St Patrick's Day to plunge flesh-meats into water and, when taken out, to dress them, eat them and call them fishes of St Patrick.'

Long after Patrick was dead and buried various 'lives' were written and a host of legends grew up that attributed amazing powers to him. Most, like the oft-told tale that he banished snakes from the island, have no historical basis. There never were any snakes native to Ireland. The earliest written source of the assertion that he used the shamrock to explain the Christian idea of the Trinity (three gods in one) dates from the eighteenth century. Soon after that it became a tradition to wear shamrock on the coat or hat and, in the evening, to drown the shamrock as a signal that the last *pota Pádraig* (St Patrick's pot) of the day had been consumed. The shamrock was placed into a glass of punch before the final toast was drunk. Then it was plucked from the bottom of the glass and thrown over the left shoulder.

IRISD FLAG

This colourful and suitably patriotic cocktail is just the thing for toasting the shamrock on St Patrick's Day

Ingredients:

1 shot crème de menthe

1 shot Baileys Cream liqueur

1 shot Hennessy brandy

Method:

This is a 'built' cocktail. Pour crème de menthe into the bottom of a highball glass. Float the Baileys on top, followed by the brandy. The result is a green, white and orange tricolour like the Irish flag.

COLCANNON

For a dish that is not widely eaten today, colcannon remains remarkably widely known. And it has the distinction of having a song dedicated to it, a song that, like the recipe itself, has two versions. If you say 'colcannon' in a crowded room in Ireland, chances are that half the room will break into one version of the song and the other half into a completely different version.

COLCANNON MADE WITH KALE:

'Did you ever eat colcannon when 'twas made with yellow cream
And the kale and praties blended like the picture in a dream?
Did you ever take a forkful and dip it in the lake
Of heather-flavoured butter that your mother used to make?
Oh you did, yes you did! So did he and so did I,
And the more I think about it sure, the more I want to cry.'

COLCANNON MADE WITH CABBAGE:

'Did you ever eat colcannon when 'twas made with thickened cream
And the greens and scallions blended like the picture in a dream?
Did you ever scoop a hole on top to hold the melting cake
Of clover-flavoured butter which your mother used to make?
Did you ever eat and eat, afraid you'd let the ring go past,
And some old married sprissman would get it at the last?'

BOTH VERSIONS END WITH:

'God be with the happy times when trouble we had not
And our mothers made colcannon in the little three-legged pot.'

Colcannon is so like champ, cally, stampy and poundies that it is difficult to understand how it ever came to have a different name. Yet, all over the country, colcannon is colcannon and known as nothing else. As in the two versions of the song, it can be made with kale or with greens – meaning cabbage. Those reared on the version made with kale don't accept the cabbage version as colcannon and those in the other camp, I'm sure, are equally insistent that their method is the true one. I was reared without the addition of scallions and feel they interfere with the very individual taste of kale. Others would maintain that they are an essential ingredient.

Whatever your preference between cabbage and kale, I suggest you use kale for your St Patrick's Day dish as it results in a green fluffy colcannon.

Ingredients:

1 kg/2½ lbs floury potatoes, peeled

250 ml/8 fl oz/1 US cup curly kale, cooked and finely chopped

250 ml/8 fl oz/1 US cup hot milk

1 bunch (about 6) scallions, finely chopped (optional)

4 tablesp butter

SERVES 6–8

Method:

Steam the potatoes until tender. Dry off by placing a clean tea-towel on top for a few minutes. Then put through a potato ricer or mouli.

Strip the soft kale leaf away from the stem and tougher veins. Discard the stem and veins. Shred the leaves finely. Bring a large, stainless-steel pot of salted water to a furious boil, add the kale leaves and cook until just tender. Drain and cool immediately under cold running water – vital if you wish to preserve its bright green colour. Drain, then squeeze out any excess liquid. Place the kale in a food processor with the hot milk and process until you have a thick green 'soup'.

Put the scallions (if using) in a small pan with the butter and soften for just 30 seconds.Lightly, but thoroughly, mix the scallions, potatoes and kale until you have a pale green fluff. Season with salt and freshly ground black pepper, then reheat until piping hot in the microwave or (covered) in an oven. Serve with more butter

CORNED BEEF

Until relatively recent times most Irish beef was exported, much of it 'on the hoof', but a great deal salted in barrels – corned beef, as we know it. This would have been the only beef that ordinary Irish people ever ate; on some feast days like Christmas a farmer might slaughter an elderly cow (one past breeding or milking) and send out a cut to his neighbours – the beef equivalent of 'the Christmas pudding round'. Corned beef is mentioned in the eleventh century dream poem Aishlinge Meic ConGlinne:

> 'Many wonderful provisions, Pieces of palatable food
> Full without fault, Perpetual joints of corned beef.'

Colcannon [see previous recipe] is the perfect accompaniment for corned beef. Traditional sauces to accompany corned (or spiced) beef and colcannon are a simple white parsley sauce or a mustard sauce.

SERVES 4–6

Ingredients:

1¼ kg/3 lb (approx) corned beef (silverside, topside, round, rump – **or** brisket which is much fattier)

1 onion

1 carrot

bouquet garni

2 cloves garlic

500 ml/1 pt/2 US cups/ (small bottle) dry cider

Method:

Soak the meat overnight in several changes of water. Place all the ingredients in a large ovenproof pot with fresh water to cover. Bring to the boil, skimming all the while. Reduce heat to a bare simmer and cover tightly. Cooked in the oven at 150°C/300°F/ Gas 2, it takes between 40 to 60 minutes per 450 g/1 lb. Tenderness varies (depending on beast, cut and cure), so test when three-quarters of the cooking time has elapsed. If you intend to eat the meat cold, as many Irish prefer, allow it to cool in the cooking water, then remove to a plate and press lightly, either in a meat press, or by covering with a plate weighed down by 2 x 400g food tins.

Easter

Preparations for Easter began on Good Friday. The eggs to be eaten on Easter Sunday were collected and marked with a cross. The practice of marking bread made on Good Friday with a cross began in medieval times and it is a custom that survives today in the hot cross bun which is always eaten on Good Friday. To this day in Ireland the traditional loaf of soda bread, whether made at home or in bakeries, is also marked with a cross. Fishing was banned on Good Friday but in coastal areas it was common to gather shellfish and edible seaweed for the main meal.

In times gone by, Easter Saturday was a favourite day for 'the whipping of the herring', a ceremony devised by butchers who suffered a severe loss of business during the long Lenten fast. A herring, the mainstay of the Lenten diet, would be tied to a post and paraded through the town to the local river. Butchers' boys armed with long rods enthusiastically whipped the herring to flitters. The remains were hurled into the river and a quarter of a young lamb, decorated with ribbons and garlands of flowers, was carried to the market place with much good humour and musical accompaniment.

Easter is now the most important festival in the Christian calendar. It replaced the pagan spring festivals of fertility at which the custom of exchanging eggs as a token of renewed life was common. In Christian times the eating and decorating of eggs became an end-of-Lent treat. Breakfast consisted of a hearty meal of eggs, six being the average for a grown man. The eggs were boiled in water dyed with natural dyes from plants. Children used to go around the houses collecting eggs and other treats forbidden during Lent and have their own little feast, roasting eggs and potatoes in a *clúdóg*, an outdoor fire. Nowadays children don't make their own feasts, and chocolate eggs have become the traditional treat.

Easter Sunday dinner was a festive meal for all those who could afford to eat meat. Well-off farmers killed a cow and sent portions to friends and poorer neighbours. But the most highly favoured dish was roast kid or young lamb and 'spring' lamb remains the most popular Easter Sunday dish today.

The Easter 'cake dance' was also a strong tradition and dates back to medieval times. In the afternoon, young people gathered at a convenient spot, usually near an ale house. The ale-wife provided the 'cake', which could be a currant loaf or a barm brack, sometimes decorated with birds, fishes and animals. This was set on top of a pike or a churn-dash and the couples danced around it to the point of exhaustion. The last couple left dancing then 'took the cake' and divided it up amongst the others.

ḋow to ḋye eggs:

Eggs boiled with raw beetroot turn a deep pinkish red, those boiled in spinach water take on a greenish colour, and if you wrap the eggs in onion skins secured with brown cotton you can achieve a mottled orange effect.

Alternatively, decorate eggs after boiling with crayons or watercolours.

ḃoꞇ ꞓꞡoss ꞏꞌꞓuꞑs

Traditionally eaten on Good Friday, the Friday before Easter Sunday. The cross on the top is the Christian symbol, a reminder that this was the day Jesus was crucified.

MAKES 12

Ingredients:
For the dough:

450 g/1 lb/4 US cups unsifted strong white flour

7 g/¼ oz/1 teasp quick-action yeast

a good pinch of salt

½ teasp ground cinnamon

1 teasp mixed spice/allspice

½ teasp nutmeg, grated

90 g/3 oz/½ US cup sultanas

90 g/3 oz/(scant) ½ US cup currants

30 g/1 oz/1 tablesp mixed peel, chopped (optional)

1 medium-sized egg, beaten

250 ml/8 fl oz/1 US cup full-fat milk

For the crosses:

2 tablesp butter

45 g/1½ oz/⅓ US cup flour

a little cold water

Method:

Mix the flour, yeast, salt, spices and dried fruit together. Add the egg and enough milk to make a soft dough (you may need more or less liquid). Knead the dough until really smooth to the touch and elastic in texture; by hand this will take 10 minutes, using dough hooks and an electric mixer rather less time (and considerably less effort). Divide into 12 pieces and shape into round buns. Place on a well-greased baking tray, leaving enough room for each bun to expand. Cover and prove at (warm) room temperature until they have risen and reached twice their original size.

Make the dough for the crosses by rubbing softened butter into flour and wetting with just enough water to make a soft dough. Roll out thinly and cut into narrow strips. Wet the underside of each strip and place two strips on each bun in the shape of a cross. Bake at 200°C/400°F/Gas 6 for 25–30 minutes They should be well-risen and browned and, when the bottom of a bun is tapped lightly, it should sound hollow. Serve freshly cooked, with butter.

woodcock smokery kippers with potato salad and poached egg

Ross Lewis, former commissioner general of Euro-Toques in Ireland, is chef and co-owner with restaurant manager Martin Corbett of Dublin's fine Chapter One restaurant. Ross created this recipe for the luncheon at which the Irish Food Writers Guild announced their Food Award winners for 2001. Sally Barnes's Woodcock Smokery kippers won an award and are spectacularly good.

SERVES 4

Ingredients:

6 baby waxy potatoes, such as Nicola or Charlotte

a little white wine vinegar

4 small eggs

4 Woodcock Smokery kippers

15 g/½ oz/1 tablesp unsalted butter

a little olive oil

1 tablesp snipped fresh chives

4 fresh chervil sprigs

For the mustard beurre blanc:

125 ml/4 fl oz/½ US cup tarragon vinegar

60 ml/2 fl oz/¼ US cup dry white wine

2 shallots, very finely chopped

60 ml/2 fl oz/¼ US cup double cream

135 g/4½ oz unsalted butter, chilled and diced

1 tablesp wholegrain mustard

½ tablesp Dijon mustard

Maldon sea salt and freshly ground black pepper

Method:

Preheat the oven to 220°C/450°F/Gas 7, or the grill to high. Place the potatoes in a pan of boiling salted water, cover and bring to the boil. Reduce the heat and simmer for 15–20 minutes until tender. Drain and leave to cool a little, then carefully peel away the skins and cut each potato into 2 even-sized rounds, discarding the rounded ends.

Heat a large deep pan two-thirds full with water and add one tablespoon of vinegar for each 1.2 litres/2 pints/1¼ US quarts of water. Bring to the boil and then break the eggs, one at a time, into where the water is bubbling. Reduce the heat and simmer gently for 3 minutes, then carefully remove the eggs with a slotted spoon into a large bowl of iced water to prevent further cooking. When cold, trim any ragged ends from the cooked egg whites.

To make the mustard beurre blanc, place the vinegar, wine and shallots in a small pan and reduce to 2 tablespoons. Stir in the cream. Reduce the heat to very low, whisk in the butter cubes, a few at a time, adding the next batch just before the butter already in the pan is entirely melted, whisking all the time. Stir in both mustards and season to taste. Keep warm over a very, very low heat.

Arrange the kippers on a baking sheet and dot with butter. Place in the oven or under the grill for 2–3 minutes until warm, then remove the skin. Keep warm. Heat the olive oil in a sauté pan, add the potato rounds, season and just warm through, tossing occasionally. Place the poached eggs in a pan of gently simmering salted water for 1 minute to heat through.

To serve, arrange three pieces of potato on each serving plate and add the kippers. Place the poached eggs on top and cover with the mustard beurre blanc. Season to taste and scatter over the chives, then garnish with the chervil sprigs.

Kipper

FRESH HERRINGS IN OATMEAL

A classic dish. The oatmeal gives a crisp coating and a nutty taste. Traditionally the humble herring languished at the bottom of the fish hierarchy – the fish of the poor, the fish of penitence, a fish that failed to inspire love. However, in coastal areas, the Irish did eat herring, especially when shoals came near the shore in September. Fresh, they were known as harvest herrings; the surplus was salted and stored in barrels to eat as a 'savour' for potatoes – first soaked in water overnight, then simmered in the pot with the potatoes. In more prosperous households they were 'soused' in beer and vinegar, or given a coating of oatmeal and fried.

SERVES 4

Ingredients:

4–8 very fresh herring fillets*

8 heaped tablesp oat flakes

2 eggs, beaten

3 tablesp plain white flour

4 tablesp butter

* as herrings vary so much in size you will have to be the judge of how many you will need from the fish available on the day.

Method:

Wash and dry the fish. Dip each one in flour first, then in egg, then in oat flakes (press the latter on to the fish). If you have time, rest in a cool place to allow this coating to set. Heat a large frying pan, add some of the butter and heat it until it begins to foam. Add the herrings and cook on one side until the oat flakes are evenly browned but not burnt. Turn with a fish slice, add extra butter if needed, and brown on the second side. If you need to cook in batches, keep the first batch warm.

Serve with wedges of lemon and grilled tomato halves.

oats

Loin of Lamb with a Sage Crust,

shallot and caper compote, confit of carrot and garlic, and baby turnip cooked in port

---

This recipe by Ross Lewis of Chapter One restaurant shows how the best Irish chefs have put a modern spin on many traditional Irish foods. The ingredients for the accompaniments, while numerous, are simple to prepare and cook and should be done before you sauté the lamb, which in Ireland is served pink and juicy.

SERVES 4

Ingredients:

4 servings of loin of spring lamb, skin removed

a little olive oil

For the sage crust:

6 slices white bread, crusts removed

4 sage leaves

15 g/½ oz parmesan cheese

1 egg yolk

60 g/2 oz butter, at room temperature

1 tablesp cream

½ teasp Dijon mustard

For the shallot and caper compote:

225 g/8 oz shallot, chopped

1 clove garlic

1 teasp chopped thyme leaves

90 ml/3 fl oz/ a generous ¼ US cup white wine

2 teasp Dijon mustard

60 ml/2 fl oz crème fraîche

1 teasp capers, chopped

2 scallions (spring onions), finely chopped

knob of butter

salt and pepper

For The confit of carrot and garlic:

8 cloves of garlic, peeled

12 small cubes of carrot, matching the garlic in size

300 ml/10 fl oz/1¼ US cups olive oil

1 bay leaf

1 sprig thyme

2 star anise

For The turnips:

8 baby turnips

300 mls/10 fl oz/1¼ US cups port

knob of butter

Method:

Season each piece of loin and sauté slowly in olive oil in a thick-bottomed pan for 3–4 minutes each side, until pink inside (meat thermometer reading 58°C). Take out and rest for 5 minutes.

Put bread and sage in a blender and blend to a crumb. Add all the other ingredients, blend until smooth. Roll out between cling film to the thickness of half a finger.

Place all ingredients for the confit of carrot and garlic into a small pot or casserole and cook over low heat until cooked soft in the middle.

For the compote, sweat the shallots, garlic and thyme in butter without colouring them. Add wine and reduce to nothing. Add Dijon and crème fraîche and cook for another 5–6 minutes over a low heat. Finish with scallion and capers. Season with salt and pepper. Form into 4 oval-shaped quenelles by pressing the mixture lightly between the bowls of two tablespoons.

Blanch the baby turnips in boiling salted water until half cooked (about 6 minutes). Peel off the skins and place the turnips into the port and finish cooking slowly. When the port is reduced to a syrup, stir in a small knob of butter and use this for the sauce.

Assembly:

Assemble the servings by cutting the crust into 4 strips and placing one on top of each piece of lamb and place under the grill until glazed. Garnish with the carrot and garlic confit, a quenelle of shallot compote (at room temperature), the baby turnip and port reduction. Serve with plain boiled potatoes.

Bealṫaine, May Day, 1 May

Bealtaine, the start of summer, was always an important day in the Irish rural calendar. Sheep began to be moved up from the home fields to summer pasture and cattle were sent to 'booley', summer grazing on moorland and mountains. It was a day of stocktaking in the house. A demonstration of good management was to have enough flour left to make one formal dish. Sir Henry Piers, a seventeenth century writer, described the usual dish as 'stirabout, or hasty pudding, that is flour and milk boiled thick'. By the early nineteenth century, Hall, who wrote *A Tour Through Ireland*, observed other, tastier dishes: 'I found that all the low people, Protestant as well as Catholic, had gone out in the morning to get syllabubs or milk cooked in a certain way and that many of them were drunk before breakfast'. Within the home, dishes featuring summer 'white meats' – like a cake made with fresh curd cheese – were common.

Between sunset on May Eve and sunrise on May Day, the *Síoge* (fairies) were believed to be on the move. They would grasp any opportunity to steal a human child (or young woman) and to leave in its place a 'changeling'. Customs designed to protect against the harmful activity of the *Sí* were practised. People stuck close to home. Strangers seen on the home property were suspected of evil intent; even strange animals were unwelcome. The general rule was: 'no spending, no lending, no borrowing' and beggars knew better than to ask for a drink of water or a light for their pipe – might they not be someone from the otherworld in disguise? Dairy produce, especially butter, was considered to be particularly vulnerable and almost anything taken from the house or farm could be used to 'steal' the butter, giving the evil-doer a greatly increased quantity while the victim's churn produced nothing but froth.

The custom of drawing blood from living cattle is documented right up to the nineteenth century. Blood was used for supplementing the diet in times of scarcity but on *Lá Bealtaine* it had ritual significance: it was believed to provide magical protection. The *Ulster Journal of Archaeology* (1855) noted: 'On May Eve the peasantry used to drive their cattle into old ring forts and raths thought to be much frequented by the fairies, bleed them, taste their blood and pour the remainder on the earth.'

CROZIER BLUE CHEESE AND SPINACH IN PUFF PASTRY

WITH APPLE AND CELERIAC PURÉE

This recipe was created by Derry Clarke, the double Michelin star chef/patron of Dublin's L'Ecrivain restaurant, for the 2005 Irish Food Writers Guild annual Good Food Awards luncheon. Crozier Blue Cheese was one of the award winners.

SERVES 4

Ingredients:

280 g/10 oz Crozier Blue cheese

255 g/9 oz fresh spinach leaves

3 shallots, peeled and chopped

4 tablesp Madeira, or medium sherry

60 ml/2 fl oz chicken stock

350–400 g/12–14 oz puff pastry

1 egg, beaten

For the purée:

200 g/7 oz celeriac, peeled and chopped finely

2 cooking apples (preferably Bramley), peeled and chopped finely

1 large floury potato, cooked and mashed while hot

1 tablesp olive oil

1 shallot, peeled and diced finely

1 clove of garlic, peeled and crushed

1 sprig thyme

100 ml/3½ fl oz/³/₈ US cup milk

100 ml/3½ fl oz/³/₈ US cup cream

Method:

Wash the spinach, blanch in boiling water, drain and chop. Set it aside. Place shallots and Madeira in a small pot; simmer until reduced by half. Add stock and simmer again until reduced by half. Add the cheese and spinach; mix, season to taste with black pepper and a little salt. Cool.

Roll out the pastry thinly (½ cm/¼ inch thick); cut into 10 cm/4 inch squares. Put a well-heaped teaspoon of filling in the middle of each square. Brush edges with beaten egg and pull in the four corners towards the centre to form a parcel; seal edges by pinching the pastry together. Brush with the remaining beaten egg and bake at 180°C/350°/gas 4 for 15 minutes or until golden brown. Serve warm, with the purée.

Apple and Celeriac Purée

Heat the olive oil and gently cook the shallot, garlic and thyme in it for five minutes. Add the chopped apple and celeriac and the milk and cream. Simmer for 10–12 minutes until tender. Whiz in a food processor, or purée in a food mill. Add the mashed potato and blend well. Season to taste with salt and black pepper.

SYLLABUB

'Bub' is an Elizabethan slang term for a bubbling drink. This dessert dates from that period and would have featured on the tables of the great houses of Ireland. Originally milk and cream was poured into glasses from a height to make the drink frothy. Folklore suggests that, having poured a layer of sweetened, spiced or herb-flavoured wine into a jug, the cow was milked directly into the jug! The dish was valued for its frothy layer and sometimes whisked egg whites were added to strengthen the froth. This version holds its shape pretty well, but should be eaten wtihin twenty-four hours.

SERVES 6

Ingredients:

300 ml/10 fl oz/1¼ US cup cream

the juice and rind of 1 large lemon

2 tablesp brandy

2 tablesp caster sugar

5 tablesp sherry

Method:

Mix everything except the cream together and stir until dissolved. Whisk the cream until it just begins to thicken. Still whisking, very slowly add the sherry mixture. Whisk until the mixture is light and fluffy.

Spoon into six, preferably flute-shaped, wine glasses. Chill for at least two hours before serving. Serve with thin ginger or almond biscuits.

Bloomsday, 16 June

Over the last thirty years this day has grown into a very significant festival for Dubliners and tourists alike. From small beginnings among enthusiasts (like the poet Patrick Kavanagh, cultural guru Anthony Cronin and novelist and satirical journalist Brian O'Nolan 'Flann O'Brien') of James Joyce's great novel *Ulysses*, which documents in detail the day of 16 June in the life of a Dublin Jew, Leopold Bloom, 'Bloomsday' has turned into an annual event.

Although now celebrated all over the world, the real festival centres upon Dublin where increasingly large numbers of people dress up in Edwardian period costume to re-enact the perambulations of Mr Bloom and his companion Stephen Dedalus around the city and to eat (and drink) what he consumed on that day, preferably having lunch in Davy Byrne's pub where Bloom ate a Gorgonzola cheese sandwich with mustard, and drank a glass of Burgundy wine. Bloom is also described as eating the inner organs of beasts and fowls but most of all he liked grilled mutton kidneys which gave to his palate 'a fine tang of faintly scented urine'. The commemorations in Dublin begin in Eccles Street near the Mater Hospital in north Dublin where Bloom lived with his wife, Molly. The James Joyce Cultural Centre in North Great George's Street is also nearby. So many people now take part on the day that to get lunch in Davy Byrne's on Bloomsday you would need to have booked a table a few years in advance! But many fine restaurants all over the city put on a special 'Bloomsday' menu.

Peter Caviston in Glasthule, near the Joyce Tower where the novel opens with Buck Mulligan and Dedalus, is a purist. The original pilgrimage of Kavanagh, Cronin and Flann O'Brien set out from Glasthule. Peter (a superb fishmonger and restaurateur) now runs a day-long street festival with a kidney-based breakfast. At lunch, after one of the restaurant's wonderful fish dishes, he serves as a dessert the very best Gorgonzola cheese he can find with the finest of Burgundy wines.

fowl Livers

If you wish to celebrate Bloomsday in a quiet, solitary way, this recipe makes a delicious breakfast dish.

SERVES 1

Ingredients:

1 shallot

1 tablesp unsalted butter

3 chicken livers (**or** 2 duck, **or** 1 goose liver)

1 tablesp Irish whiskey

2 slices wholemeal bread, toasted

Method:

Soften a shallot (or half a small onion) over a low heat in unsalted Irish butter; turn up the heat, add the liver of a few chickens, a duck, or a goose (fat, membrane and tubes carefully removed), and sear it until it is browned on the outside and is firm, but still pink, in the centre. Then season it and flame it, briefly, on the pan in a tablespoon of whiskey. Eat at once on toasted wholemeal bread.

Devilled Kidneys

Leopold would not have gone to this trouble for his wife, Molly. However, this is a wonderful dish that she would undoubtedly have adored.

SERVES 4

Ingredients:

4 lamb kidneys, skinned, membranes removed, cut in half horizontally, with tubes and white fat cores removed; then washed and dried

½ tablesp mango chutney

¼ tablesp mustard powder

2–3 drops Tabasco sauce

I teasp olive oil

½ level teasp Demerara sugar

I tablesp lemon juice

a pinch of cayenne pepper

15 g/½ oz unsalted butter

½ level teasp tomato purée

I teasp chopped fresh parsley

½ a small red chilli, deseeded and cut into shreds (optional)

Method:

Mix the chutney and mustard, the Tabasco sauce, oil, sugar, lemon juice and cayenne pepper together in a shallow dish. Add the kidneys and toss to coat. Cover with foil and refrigerate for two hours. Heat the grill, lined with foil, to medium and grill the kidneys for about 10 minutes, brushing them regularly with the marinade. Blend the butter with tomato purée and chopped parsley. Serve the kidneys topped with this sauce, the thinly sliced chillies (optional) and the grilled half tomatoes. Eat with good bread to mop up the juices.

Midsummer

The summer solstice is 21 June. However, it was common in early Christian times to transfer pagan festive days to the nearest Christian feast – in this case, that of St John the Baptist on 24 June. As a result, midsummer eve celebrations to mark the coming of the longest day of the year took place in most parts of Ireland on 23 June. While the customs are of pagan origin – with bonfires and ceremonies associated with protecting animals, crops and humans from harm – the bonfires were also known as *Tine Féile Eoin* (St John's Fire).

There are two fire traditions: one is a large communal fire, for a townland or village, the other, smaller fires lit by every household. The belief was that fire could protect against natural disease as well as magical influence. So the family fire was placed so that the smoke could drift over important crops and the fields in which their cattle grazed. The embers were scattered in the four corners of each field, the cattle were herded together and driven though the smoke or over the embers. A charred stick would be placed in the dairy or, in a typically Irish way of mingling pagan and Christian beliefs, used to mark a cross on dairy and byre doors.

The tradition of combining ancient and modern continues with the collecting of St John's Wort (*hypericum perforatum*) also known as 'the fairy herb'. When crushed, it has a strong odour that is said to protect against the evils of witchcraft. In Irish herbal lore it's a cure for rheumatism, wounds, and the fairy fit (an attack of depression).

The vast communal bonfires were lit as night fell. Everyone, from the smallest child to the oldest men and women, took part in the celebrations with music, dancing and the eating of simple foods like potatoes roasted in the fire ashes, with home-distilled poitín to drink. The younger boys would snatch the hot potatoes and throw them up in the air. The custom of young men and sometimes young couples jumping over the fire was partly bravado and partly the belief that it brought health, long life and protection against the evil eye.

In coastal fishing districts Midsummer Day is the time when summer fishing begins. Inland it's a time when the much-favoured sea trout may enter the rivers. In County Antrim the salmon fishermen of the River Bush hold a communal meal known as the 'Salmon Dinner'. The menu is always fish soup, freshly caught salmon, new potatoes and Bushmills whiskey. All over the island it was a day for fairs, which were as much about merriment as about buying and selling. At some fairs a high decorated pole, known as a *craebh*, was erected; attached to the top was a pair of garters and a basket of gingerbread. Musicians played and couples danced to win the prize of the garters and gingerbread cakes – the man got the garters and the women the gingerbread.

fResh cheese with soft summer fruits

Once this dish would have been made at home from cooked buttermilk and a little fresh cream. Today fresh curd cheese is soft, smooth, creamy, delicate in taste and rather lighter in texture than commercial cream cheeses. In Ireland it may be made from cows' or goats' milk.

SERVES 4

Ingredients:

225 g/8 oz/1 US cup fresh curd cheese

450 g/1 lb/3 US cups strawberries or raspberries, **or** loganberries, **or** soft fruit of your choice, washed, hulled, and (if necessary) sliced

2–3 tablesp fresh cream

2 tablesp caster sugar

Method:

Beat the cheese, cream and sugar together until well mixed. Set some fruit aside for decoration. If you're using strawberries, slice them thinly. In a serving dish (or individual serving dishes, or glasses) layer the fruit with the cheese mixture. Top with the whole fruits. Chill before serving.

whole poached salmon

Almost mandatory on an Irish buffet table, this is usually served very decoratively, with its skin and scales replaced by very finely sliced cucumber slices (time-consuming, but undoubtedly charming to look at).

SERVES 10–20 depending on weight of fish

Method:

Take one whole salmon. Lay the fish on its side in a fish kettle (on a strip of foil or muslin to enable you to lift it out easily). Pour over just enough water or vegetable stock (add a little drinkable dry white wine, if you like) to barely cover. Over a low heat bring it slowly to a bare simmer. Then, if the fish is to be eaten cold, turn off the heat and let the fish cool in the liquid before lifting it out. Before it is completely cold, skin it by slitting the skin along the back and peeling it away.

If the fish is to be eaten hot, continue simmering for 10 minutes for the first kilo/2¼ lb, 15 minutes for the second, and 20 minutes for the third. The flesh should be just opaque at the bone and you should be able to easily push a thin skewer into the thickest part of the fish.

The Wexford Strawberry Festival

For more than thirty-five years, a Strawberry Festival has been held in early July in Enniscorthy, County Wexford, a town in the heart of the sunny south-east of Ireland. The Irish weather forecasting service stands over the fact that this region is drier and sunnier – in a typical year it enjoys up to five hundred more hours of sunshine than other regions of the island. This microclimate, of course, is the reason why it's an area known for the excellence of its cultivated strawberries and other soft fruits. In the native woodlands, hedgerows and ditches, wild woodland strawberries of intense flavour and sweetness flourish and have done so since ancient times. You can still pick these but you need a sharp eye and a lot of patience.

Because the Irish love strawberries, free-fruiting varieties are now cultivated throughout the island and growing techniques have been perfected. The season now runs from April to the end of October. But there is still nothing to beat the flavour and texture of a field strawberry grown in a soil and climate that suits it – summer in County Wexford – that's what everyone celebrates. A strawberry ball is held in Enniscorthy to introduce the Strawberry Queen, there are street entertainments, arts events, and, of course, strawberries to eat on-the-go are on sale all over this exceptionally pretty town overlooking the River Slaney.

MONFIN HOUSE STRAWBERRY ALMOND TARTLETS

Chris and Avril Stewart take guests in their wonderful, classic Georgian house just outside Enniscorthy, County Wexford. Avril provided me with this recipe which is a great favourite at Monfin during the Wexford strawberry season.

MAKES 8

Ingredients:

For the pastry:

225 g/8 oz butter

100 g/3½ oz caster sugar

2 egg yolks

350 g/12 oz plain flour, sifted

100 g/3½ oz ground almonds

For the filling:

250 ml/8 fl oz/1 US cup milk

3 egg yolks

60 g/2 oz caster sugar

15 g/½ oz flour

10 g/¼ oz cornflour

vanilla essence

700 g/1½ lb fresh strawberries

5 tablesp redcurrant jelly, melted

toasted almonds

Method:

Cream together the butter and sugar until light and fluffy. Beat in the egg yolks. Gradually stir in the flour and ground almonds, and knead to a smooth dough. Cover with cling film and chill for one hour in the fridge.

Grease eight loose-bottomed 10cm/4 inch tartlet tins. Divide the dough into eight pieces and roll each one out into a circle. Line the tartlet tins with the pastry and prick the surface of each with a fork. Line each one with baking parchment and fill with baking beans or equivalent.

Bake the pastry 'blind' in an oven preheated to 190°C/375°F/Gas 5 for 15 minutes. Remove the parchment paper and beans and return pastry cases to oven to bake for 3–4 minutes longer, or until they are golden brown. Cool them in their tins on a wire tray.

Filling:

Bring the milk to the boil and set aside. Whisk the sugar and egg yolks until pale in colour. Mix in the flour and cornflour and whisk until smooth. Pour on the milk and mix well. Return the mixture to the pan and stir continuously over a medium heat until the mixture comes slowly to the boil. Continue to stir and cook for 2 minutes. The mixture will go lumpy but just remove it from the heat, keep stirring madly, and it will go smooth. Allow to cool very slightly before mixing in the vanilla essence. If the cream is too thick add a little milk to thin it out. Pour the mixture into the pastry cases and smooth. Allow to cool.

Reserve eight of the best strawberries. Hull and slice the remainder and arrange the slices in rings on top of the filling. Spoon the melted redcurrant jelly over the strawberries and leave to set in the fridge. Just before serving, place one of the reserved strawberries in the middle of each tartlet and sprinkle with toasted, sliced almonds.

The Twelfth of July

In the province of Ulster, the 'Twelth' (no 'f' words up there) is the day which celebrates the victory in 1690 of William of Orange over King James II of England at the Battle of the Boyne. The Orange Order, a Protestant, political society dedicated to 'sustaining the glorious and immortal memory of King William' was instituted in 1795. The 'Twelth' is the biggest day in their social calendar and is a local, community-based celebration. Members of the local Orange Lodge assemble and, led by their own and visiting bands, march along their route to 'the field' where, following oratory, there is singing, music, liquid refreshment and a modest feast. Nowadays the food is most often sold from mobile fast-food outlets but until the late 1960s the catering was a communal effort to raise money. In many parts of the east of the province the young people were encouraged to prepare and sell picnic-packs in the field to raise funds for their church. Typically, the pack would contain a meat paste and an egg sandwich, a sausage roll and two sweet pastries.

In the west of the province the food was prepared by local women and sold from stalls. Preparations began the night before. The men set up stalls and, as soon as the children were abed, the women would come together to prepare the traditional foods: the makings of a 'meat tea': meat, egg and salad sandwiches, and sweet Paris buns. Meat would be cooked, minced, then moistened and flavoured with a jellied stock before being cooled and then used as a spread for filling sandwiches. As well as 'sit down meat teas' (cold slices of ham and beef with a salad) most stalls used to sell a pack of two 'meat paste' sandwiches and a Paris bun in a paper bag with the corners twirled into two 'lugs' (ears) to keep it secure. Quantities of these bags, prepared in advance, were packed into laundry baskets and transported to the field along with tanks of milk, water, and the fuel to power the cookers (usually gas) to make tea. Some lodges would supply ice cream in cones, or jelly and custard. Custard powder and jelly would be farmed out to many local women and the puddings were made by the enamel bucket-full, stored overnight in a shop fridge, then transported to the field on the day to be served in dainty glass trifle dishes.

potted hough

Hough is the Scottish name for the leg or shin of beef and this or a similar recipe would have been the basis for many of the meat spreads made to fill sandwiches on 'The Twelth' in the Northern counties of Ireland. It is delicious, keeps well, freezes well, and makes you wonder why people do not buy cheap cuts of meat any more. The inclusion of a pig's trotter helps it set better.

SERVES 8–10

Ingredients:

1 kg/2¼ lbs boneless shin beef

1 marrowbone, sawn in half

1 pig's trotter (optional)

2 large carrots, peeled

1 bay leaf

1 large onion, peeled and studded with half a dozen cloves

½ teasp ground mace

a pinch of cayenne pepper

a pinch of ground ginger

salt and freshly ground black pepper

Method:

Put the meat, marrowbone and trotter (if using) into a stockpot with the carrots and the onion. Cover with cold water and bring to a gentle simmer, skimming off any grey scum that rises. Simmer for 3–4 hours until the meat is completely tender. Remove the meat from the water and refrigerate. Remove the bone and vegetables and cool the stock (ideally overnight) in the fridge, then remove the fat from the surface.

Warm the stock again and strain it thoroughly. Boil it hard until it has reduced by half. It should taste beefy but not too rich. Pass the cold beef, the meat and some of the meat and skin from the pig's trotter though a coarse mincer. Transfer to a mixing bowl and moisten with up to two ladles of the stock (you want to keep it soft and spreadable). Season with the spices and the salt and pepper, tasting as you go; mix well. Pile into a terrine dish (don't press it down too much) and ladle over just enough stock to cover the meat. Place it to set in the fridge.

Lughnasa, August

Lugh, the sun god, god of light and genius, was one of the principal gods of the *Tuatha Dé Danann*, the people of Anu, the mother of the gods. They are said to have been the fourth of six prehistoric colonisers of Ireland, arriving about four thousand years ago. From the northern islands of Greece they brought with them skills in druidry, prophesy and magic. *Lughnasa*, Lugh's festival, took place over several weeks (usually in early August) marking the beginning of the harvest and the ripening of the fruits of the earth. It was the duty of a local king to hold an assembly and an *óeanach* (a fair) for the people of his *tuath* (tribe). The most prominent of these was convened by the King of Tara who was *Ard Rí* (High King) of Ireland. According to the ancient texts, as well as a market for food and for livestock, there was a 'great market of foreigners' where gold and fine raiments could be bought.

In addition to buying and selling, the fairs featured horse racing, athletic contests, music and storytelling. Some of the ancient pagan assembly sites subsequently became places of Christian pilgrimage. Some still survive, like Croagh Patrick in County Mayo, where there is still an annual, penitential pilgrimage to the top of the mountain. In other places, the pagan practice of climbing hills to gather *fraughans*, wild blueberries, to offer to Lugh in thanks for the first wild fruits, continued. It was a day when young people in particular climbed up local mountains to take part in feasting, games, trials of strength and courting. In the evening the *Lughnasa* fire would be lit and dancing was held around it. The *fraughans* were made into cakes or tarts. After the potato was introduced into Ireland *Lughnasa* became the time when the first new potatoes were dug up and eaten, flavoured with herbs. People still gather *fraughans* in August, but one of the few survivals of the *Lughnasa* tradition is the Fraughan Festival held in Glencullen, County Wicklow, in early August.

The last remaining descendent of the Celtic assemblies and fairs is the Old Lammas Fair held every year in Ballycastle, County Antrim, in the last week of August. The Christianised name for the festival of Lugh was Lammas, or loaf mass, when loaves of bread baked from the first grains of the harvest were placed upon an altar. The fair still attracts thousands of people. Nowadays it features traditional music, horse trading and stall-holders selling edible seaweeds like dillisk (dulse), and Yellowman, a sweet toffee, pulled with the hands to give it a honeycombed texture.

'At the auld Lammas Fair, were you ever there?
Were you ever at the fair of Ballycastle-O?
Did you treat your Mary Ann to dulse and Yellaman?
At the Auld Lammas Fair of Ballycastle-O.'

yellowman, or 'yallaman'

MAKES ABOUT 1 KILO

Ingredients:

110 g/4 oz butter

30 ml/2 tablesp vinegar

225 g/8 oz treacle

225 g/8 oz golden syrup

450 g/1 lb Demerara sugar

½ teasp bicarbonate of soda, sieved

Method:

Grease a baking tin 25 cm x 25 cm (10 inch x 10 inch). Melt the butter in a pan and add the vinegar, treacle, syrup and sugar. Stir over a gentle heat until all the sugar has dissolved; then raise the heat and bring the mixture to the boil. Boil steadily until it reaches the soft crack stage (151°C/304°F on a sugar thermometer). You can test this by dropping a small amount of the mixture into a saucer of cold water; if it is ready it should become crisp. Remove from the heat and stir in the bicarbonate of soda. When it foams up, stir again and then pour onto the greased baking tin. Now, using a spatula, keep working the edges into the centre until the mixture is pale. Allow to cool and mark up into squares, or break into chunks when hard.

ÐINGLE PIES

Pies were made for special occasions in Dingle, County Kerry: for Lughnasa, for Lady Day in September, and November Day (Feast of All Saints). They were also made for fair days, when nobody had time to sit down to a proper meal, so the pie shops flourished. They provided a sustaining snack for the farmers and fishermen. The pies were made from scraps of mutton or the meat of a sheep's head (Dingle is close to mountainous sheep country). There were several recipes for mutton pies in and around Dingle. All are very simple. Fishermen brought them to sea in a can and heated them up in mutton stock over a little fire made in a tin box at the bottom of the boat. A cold baked pie was better for the farmer's pocket.

MAKES 6 SMALL PIES

Ingredients:

450 g/1lb boneless mutton or lamb (fat and gristle removed)

1 large onion, peeled and diced

2 carrots, diced

1 potato, peeled and diced

2 sticks celery, diced

1 egg, beaten

salt and ground black pepper

For the shortcrust pastry:

500 g/1¼ lb plain flour

255 g/9 oz butter (or half and half butter and white vegetable fat)

120 ml/4 fl oz very cold water

Method:

Make the pastry by sieving the flour into a large bowl, then rub the butter (and/or fat) into the flour with your fingertips (or a pastry blender) aerating it as much as possible. Add the chilled water. Mix with a knife or fork until the mixture clings together. Turn out onto a floured worktop and knead lightly once or twice until smooth. Wrap in baking parchment or foil and leave to relax in the refrigerator for 20 minutes.

Mix all the filling ingredients together in a large bowl, and season them well. If you have any lamb gravy left over from a roast add a little to the mixture; it makes it juicier.

Preheat the oven to 180°C/350°F/Gas 4.

Cut a third off the pastry to make the pie lids. Roll out the rest. Use a small plate as a guide, (re-rolling the pastry as necessary) cut out six circles. Divide the filling mixture between the circles, piling it in the middle of each. Roll out the remaining pastry and cut out six smaller circles about 10 cm/4 inches across. Lay these on top. Dampen the edges of the bases and bring up around the filling, pleating to fit the lid, and pinch the edges together. Make a small hole in the top of each pie to let out the steam. Brush the pies with beaten egg, slide on to baking sheets and bake in the preheated oven for one hour. Serve hot or cold.

FRAUGHAN FOOLS

Fraughans, or blueberries, are a secretive berry; they hide beneath the leaves of the low-growing wild plant. This recipe stretches a small amount successfully.

SERVES 4

Ingredients:

310 g/11 oz fraughans (or blueberries)

75 g/2½ oz caster sugar, or to taste

juice of 1 lemon

125 ml/4 fl oz double cream

60 ml/2 fl oz mascarpone cheese

1–2 tablesp water

Method:

Place the fraughans in a pot with the water and cook over a gentle heat until just soft. Reserve a few of the whole berries. Purée the berries with the sugar in a food processor. Pass the purée through a fine sieve; the resulting purée should be thick. Add the lemon juice, taste, and adjust to taste with sugar.

Whisk the cream until it holds soft peaks, then gently whisk in the mascarpone cheese. Fold two-thirds of the fraughan purée into this mixture. Add the reserved berries to the remaining purée and divide most of this into four wine glasses. Divide half of the cream, cheese and fraughan mixture between the glasses. Spoon a thin layer of the remaining fraughan purée on top of this. Finish with another layer of the creamy mixture. Chill. Serve with hazelnut biscuits.

GERRY GALVIN'S SMOKED EEL AND MUSSEL HOTPOT

For many years Gerry Galvin and his wife Marie ran one of Ireland's finest restaurants at Drimcong House, Moycullen, County Galway. This splendid, hot fish broth of Gerry's contains dillisk (dulse), a seaweed found all around the Irish coast and particularly associated with the Old Lammas Fair in Ballycastle.

SERVES 4

Ingredients:

60 g/2 oz dried dillisk, soaked in cold water

48 plump mussels, scrubbed and de-bearded

150 mls/5 fl oz/²/₃ US cup dry white wine

900 ml/20 fl oz/3¾ US cups fish stock

350 g/12 oz smoked eel, skinned, filleted and cut into small pieces

3 tablesp chopped sweet cicely herb

3 tablesp grated Irish farmhouse cheese (ideally Gabriel or Desmond)

salt and freshly ground black pepper

Method:

Shred the soaked dillisk. Steam the mussels in a large pot with the white wine; shell them. Strain the cooking liquor. Bring the fish stock to the boil, add the mussel liquor, the eel, shelled mussels and dillisk. Simmer for a minute. Season to taste with salt and pepper. Divide between six deep serving bowls, sprinkle with sweet cicely and cheese and serve with freshly baked soda bread.

The Galway Oyster Festival

First held in 1954 at Clarenbridge pier alongside the oyster beds, just a short distance from Galway city, this September festival has grown into a week-long celebration, now rated as one of the twelve best festivals in the world. In 1984 the festival moved to Galway city in honour of their quincentennial. As well as various cultural events, music and dancing, there are hotly-contested oyster-opening competitions, and oyster banquets at which vast quantities of oysters are consumed, washed down by the traditional accompaniment of Guinness.

CLARENBRIDGE OYSTERS
IN A PARCEL WITH SAMPHIRE & BLACK PUDDING

From Tim O'Sullivan, Head Chef at Renvyle House Hotel in County Galway, once home to a Gaelic chieftain and to Oliver St John Gogarty. With its own lake and close to one of the best salmon fisheries in the country, it is famed for its fish and shellfish dishes.

SERVES 4

Ingredients:

24 oysters

225 g/8 oz samphire

4 large round bread rolls

150 ml/5 fl oz white wine

175 g/6 oz butter

5 small leeks, finely chopped

3 tablesp double cream

2 tablesp chopped chives

150 g/5 oz black pudding, finely chopped

Method:

Preheat oven to 200°C/400°F/Gas 6. In a large pan melt 150 g/ 5 oz of the butter, add leeks, pudding and samphire. Cook for 3–4 minutes. Add wine and chives, cook for a further minute. Add the cream, simmer for 1–2 minutes. Remove from heat and keep warm.

Cut a thin slice from the top of the bread rolls, scoop out the inside and brush the cavity with the remaining butter. Put rolls on a baking tray and bake for 5–6 minutes.

Open the oysters and remove the flesh and juices. Add to the leek and pudding mix and cook for 2 minutes. Season with salt and black pepper. Fill the hot rolls with the oyster mixture, partly cover with the lids and serve with a glass of Irish stout.

Michaelmas, 29 September, Feast of St Michael the Archangel

It was the coming of the Normans and their legal customs that made Michaelmas an important date in the Irish calendar. Within 'the Pale' (the Norman's sphere of influence in Ireland) it became one of two annual rent days and it was also a day on which mayors were elected, grazing rights were let, and servants hired.

Michaelmas marked *Fomhar na nGéan* (the goose harvest) when geese hatched in the spring were ready for the markets which had been established by Normans in many towns in Ireland. In some parts of the country a goose rent rather than a cash transaction was paid at Michaelmas. In the early fourteenth century, ten geese were worth about twenty modern pence!

The care and selling of all fowl and eggs was woman's business and the money earned was spent by them too. So they would go off to market, sell their geese and then buy delicacies imported from countries with drier, warmer climates – dried fruit and spices. Strong farmers with large flocks made presents of geese to friends and often gave them to poor families as well. The goose has always been highly prized as a festive food. By far the most popular custom associated with the day was the eating of the Michaelmas goose for dinner.

Not everyone was happy about the way the goose took over the day. In Tramore, County Wexford (a seaside resort for over two hundred years), the vendors of fish, dillisk, periwinkles and other delicacies used to march to the strand and throw an effigy named *Micil* (*Michael*) into the water, just to let the archangel know that, while the whole country enjoyed their Michaelmas goose, they were losing money.

In Ireland, goose and apples are inseparable. The apple is native to Ireland and had been cultivated in orchards since monasteries were established in early Christian times. The Normans introduced new varieties and established many new orchards within the Pale. Michaelmas was the time to pick apples and make cider. Traditionally goose was eaten on two days of the year, at Michaelmas and at Christmas; believe it or not, goose once vied with beef as the main dish served on Christmas Day.

Nothing of the goose was wasted. Its quills were made into writing implements and fishing floats, the down and feathers were used in mattresses and pillows, and its fat (goose grease) was rubbed onto the chest as a cure for 'chestiness'. This remedy was still in use when I was a child. Recently it was suggested to me by a countrywoman as a cure for tennis elbow, or for tendonitis of any kind. I've also seen this wonderful fat wasted on a big black kitchen range to 'bring up the shine'.

Goose has declined as a Christmas food, replaced by the cheaper intensively-reared turkey. In the past, a goose would have been cooked in a bastible oven with cider and apples. Nowadays it is an expensive luxury. However, goose fat is wonderful for cooking potatoes in for the rest of the year.

ϻichaelϻas roast goose

Young birds under six months old were always considered a delicacy; being lean and less fatty than mature birds; they were suitable for roasting.

SERVES 6–8

Ingredients:

1 goose (about 4.5k g/10 lb), with giblets

1 onion, sliced

2 carrots, sliced

2 celery sticks, sliced

a small bunch of parsley and thyme

75 ml/2½ fl oz/a generous ¼ US cup dry cider

1 tablesp plain flour

watercress or parsley to garnish

Method:

Cover the giblets with cold water in a pan with the onion, carrots, celery and herbs. Season, then simmer for 35–40 minutes to make a stock for the gravy. Strain the stock. Preheat oven to 200°C/400°F/Gas 6.

Wipe out the goose and stuff the neck cavity of the bird with the potato stuffing from the next recipe. Weigh the stuffed goose and calculate the cooking time at 15 minutes per 450g/1lb and 15 minutes over. Always allow at least another 20 minutes' resting time when calculating the time at which you will serve the goose. Prick the skin all over with a fork, sprinkle generously with salt and pepper and rub these in well. Put the goose on a rack in a large roasting pan, cover with foil and put it into the preheated oven.

After an hour, remove the goose from the oven and pour off the fat that has accumulated in the roasting pan (reserve this in a jar in the fridge for roasting potatoes). Pour the dry cider over the goose and return to the oven. Half an hour before the end of the estimated cooking time remove the foil and baste the bird with the juices. Return to the oven, uncovered, and allow the bird to brown and the skin to crisp. When cooked, transfer to a heated serving dish and put it in a warm place to rest for about 20 minutes.

Make the gravy by pouring off any excess fat from the roasting pan, leaving only about two tablespoons. Sprinkle in enough plain flour to absorb this and cook over a medium heat for a minute or so, scraping up the sediments on the bottom of the pan. Stir in enough giblet stock to make a gravy, bring it to the boil and, stirring constantly, simmer for a few minutes. Add any juices that have accumulated under the resting bird, season to taste, and pour the gravy into a heated sauceboat.

Remove the potato stuffing from the goose into a heated bowl. Carve the goose into slices, mixing breast and leg. Serve goose and stuffing garnished with watercress or chopped parsley and the gravy.

POTATO STUFFING

In Kerry this stuffing is known as 'pandy'. No goose is complete without a generous amount of potato stuffing to soak up some of the gorgeous fat. The herb you choose is up to you. If the stuffing is for pork, goose or duck, fresh sage is traditional; thyme, winter savoury and parsley are other possibilities, either singly or mixed.

Ingredients:

900 g/2 lbs floury potatoes, cooked, dried and mashed

450 g/1 lb onion, peeled and chopped

2 large apples, peeled, cored and chopped (optional)

225 g/½ lb lean sausage meat (optional)

1 tablesp butter, or goose fat, or duck fat

2 tablesp fresh herbs, finely chopped

Method:

Put the potatoes in a large mixing bowl. Melt the butter or goose fat in a pan and in it sweat the chopped onion and apple. Pan-fry the sausage meat, breaking it up with a fork until browned and cooked through. Add the onion, apple, cooked sausage meat (if using) and herbs to the potatoes. Season to taste with salt (very little if you are using sausage meat) and freshly ground black pepper. Cool stuffing thoroughly. Stuffing is best made the day before roasting the goose.

Harvest Home

The exact day on which the end of the harvest was celebrated depended on local crops and, naturally, the weather. Grains had to be gathered without delay when ripe lest they be damaged by disease or by grain fall from the stalk. At harvest time everyone was called upon to help; women and children, friends and neighbours gathered in a *meitheal*. The last area of grain left standing in a field was a symbol of the end of the harvest and a ceremony was made of the cutting these last sheaves.

The exact nature of this ceremony varied from region to region. Small animals, rabbits, often hares, took refuge in the last area of uncut grain and in many parts of Ireland the workers gathered round and raised a shout to 'put the hare out'. If a neighbouring farm had grain left unreaped, the hare was always believed to head for there. In folk tradition this hare turned into a 'hag', a being from the otherworld capable of a variety of evil deeds. Having the hag as a resident was deeply undesirable because hags stole cows' milk and the farmer who was last to cut his corn had to support her for the following year.

The last sheaf was tied in an ornamental fashion and carried to the door of the farmhouse. There the workers demanded a treat, either drinks there and then, or the promise of a 'harvest home' – a feast given by the farmer for workers, both paid and voluntary. In small farms it would be a few drinks in the kitchen, in large ones it would be held in a cleared-out barn furnished for the evening with tables, chairs and benches, and decorated with sheaves of corn.

There would be an elaborate meal and plentiful drinks, followed by a dance. Boiled bacon and cabbage, roast ribs of beef, or corned beef, were followed by a steamed fruit pudding or a harvest fruit loaf, all washed down with home-brewed beer or cider (and, when available, locally-made *poitín*). Then everyone trooped outside to allow the barn to be cleared for the harvest dance. Large bowls of punch were provided, the health of all present (and absent) would be drunk and the music performed by local singers and instrumentalists would go on (with intervals) into the wee small hours.

In areas where the land was too poor to grow grain and during the period when the potato was the dominant food of the poor, the end of the potato harvest was celebrated by a 'stampy' party for workers and helpers. It was so called because the main dish was stampy (a dish also called boxty) which consists of mixed grated raw potatoes and cooked potatoes, sometimes bound with flour. On special occasions, like harvest home, additional flavourings were sometimes added: caraway seeds, sugar and cream. This much less elaborate harvest dish was followed by a 'stampy dance'.

STAMPY, CHAMP, POUNDIES, CALLY AND PANDY

All of these dishes are variations on boiled, mashed potatoes with additions. The additions are most commonly members of the onion family – chives, scallions (spring onions) or ordinary onions. In the northern counties champ is also the name given to various other mixtures of mashed potatoes with beans, peas, parsley or nettles.

Ingredients:

1 kilo/2–2½ lb of potatoes

1 cup chopped scallions (spring onions)

1 cup milk

butter

Method:

Prepare boiled potatoes and while they are drying prepare the scallions. Chop the scallions, including the green leaves, and simmer them in the milk for a few minutes. Keep them warm while you 'pound' the potatoes.

A 'pounder' was a heavy block of wood on a long handle. It was used, often by the man of the house, to pound or stamp the spuds. Remember that it was quite usual in those days to cook half a stone (3k/7lb) of potatoes for each person, so this could be quite heavy work. Whatever modern appliance you use it is essential to have a purée of potatoes completely free from lumps. Add the scallions and the milk to the mashed potatoes, season well with salt and freshly ground black pepper and mix them together thoroughly. You may add more milk if the mixture is not creamy enough but on no account add so much that they become wet.

Champ should be served piping hot, so you may be need to reheat the potatoes at this point. Serve on very hot plates. Make a 'dunt' in the top of the potatoes. This is for your butter which melts into a little lake on the top so that you can dip each spoonful of potato into it. Champ was a dish in itself but nowadays it is quite usual to serve it as an accompaniment to grilled sausages or boiled bacon. It is a perfect accompaniment for all kinds of fish.

Chives, small young nettle-tops, peas, broad beans, or 4–5 heaped tablespoons of chopped fresh parsley can be substituted for the scallions in this recipe. The peas or beans are cooked first in the milk and can then be just added to the mashed potatoes or mashed in with the potatoes.

"beetle"

BLACKBERRY AND APPLE CRUMBLE

Fruit crumbles are quicker to prepare than tarts or pies. Apples head the list, followed closely (when in season) by a combination of blackberries and apple, rhubarb, plums, and gooseberries. Use cooking apples rather than dessert apples. A variety called Bramley is best as it cooks to a fluffy texture and has a great taste. The addition of oatflakes is traditional and gives an especially crunchy crumble topping.

Ingredients:

700 g/1½ lb cooking apples (or fruit of your choice)

225 g/8 oz blackberries

110 g/4 oz/generous ½ US cup sugar (or to taste)

a few cloves, or ½ teasp freshly ground nutmeg

For the crumble:

110 g/4 oz/1 US cup unsifted plain white flour

60 g/2 oz/²/₃ US cup oatflakes

90 g/3 oz butter, chopped

90 g/3 oz/scant ½ US cup light brown sugar

Method:

Peel, core and slice the apples into wedges. Place in an oval or rectangular pie dish with the blackberries. Sprinkle the sugar and spice on top. If you have a sweet tooth use the full amount. Rub the butter into the flour. Add the sugar and oatflakes and mix well, pressing it lightly together. Spread this evenly over the fruit. Bake at 180°C/350°F/Gas 4 for 40–45 minutes or until the crumble is golden brown and the fruit tender. Serve hot with whipped cream.

Alternative crumble topping:

175 g/6 oz/1½ US cups unsifted plain flour

90 g/3 oz butter

90 g/3 oz/scant ½ cup Demerara sugar

60 g/2 oz/½ cup walnuts, chopped

Rub the butter into the flour and then mix in the sugar and chopped walnuts. Spread on top of filling and press down lightly.

Hallowe'en, 31 Осто฿ек, and Saเจhaเก, 1 Noveเจ฿ек

The ancient Celtic festival of *Samhain* is on 1 November and the eve of that day – Hallowe'en, is still celebrated all over Ireland with bonfires, special foods and general merrymaking, especially among the children.

For the Celts, *Samhain* marked the end of their agricultural year. Basically this was when they battened down the hatches for the winter! The herds were gathered in and animals which were not to be kept for breeding were killed. Some were eaten fresh at a great feast but most were preserved by salting or cured by smoking. It was a time for making sacrifices to the Celtic gods to ensure good fortune in the coming year.

In Irish mythology *Samhain* was one of a number of times in the year when the barriers between the natural world and the otherworld broke down and encounters between mortals and the *sióge* (fairies) were likely because the fairies were out and about in great numbers. Efforts to Christianise this festival were only partially successful. In the Christian calendar, 1 November was designated All Saints' Day and Hallowe'en was called All Souls' Night, when people were encouraged to pray for the dead, but *Samhain* remained an essentially pagan festival. In many areas the old name *Oíche na Sprideanna* (the night of the spirits) persisted because of the belief that both the fairies and the ghosts of the dead were active that night. So, while people would say they were leaving out food for dead ancestors, the practice did double duty as food to appease the *sióge*, especially the dark and sullen *púca* (Shakespeare's Puck) who was believed to be at his most mischievous at this period.

This blending of pagan and Christian customs grew into the 'guisers' or 'vizards' – groups of boys and young men disguised by masks who travelled around seeking contributions towards the Hallowe'en party. This tradition survives in the Hallowe'en masks and costumes worn by small children today to turn them into witches and fairies, or ghosts and skeletons, which are similar to ones on display in the National Museum. In the early evening the youngsters go 'round the houses' and you're considered a poor sport if you don't have a stock of apples and nuts and other goodies to give them for the Hallowe'en feast held outdoors around a bonfire.

The main festive dish from Celtic times was *banb-amna* (the piglet of *Samhain*). Then, a few centuries ago, the Christian feast day was declared a day of abstinence on which no meat was to be eaten. Thus a new set of traditional dishes emerged and these are the ones we eat today: potato and herb dishes like colcannon and stampy, cakes flavoured for the occasion with caraway seeds, sugar and cream, apple cakes and dumplings, barm brack, and fresh nuts and apples. Charms were often placed in some of these dishes. Finding one foretold the future: a ring meant marriage before the spring, a dried pea or a thimble heralded spinsterhood, a button batchelordom, a bean offered riches, a bit of rag poverty, and a chip of wood (or a matchstick) meant that your husband (or wife) would beat you.

These charms are a faint echo of divination games once widely played at Hallowe'en. Four plates would be laid on a table; into one was placed a ring, into another a grain of wheat or barley, one was filled with water, another with clay. In turn each person would be blindfolded and led to the table. The plates were shuffled after the blindfold was put on. Depending on which plate the victim placed their hand, so was their future foretold. The water meant migration, the ring marriage, the grain prosperity, and the clay death.

Most of the games, however, related to love and courtship. For example, two hazelnuts or walnuts (sometimes just two grains of wheat) were placed on the embers of the fire and named after a couple deemed to be courting. Depending on whether they smouldered away quietly or jumped apart, so would the couple whose names they carried. It was believed that an apple, peeled so that the skin remained in one long unbroken strip, would form the initial of a future sweetheart when it fell to the ground.

BARM BRACK

There are two versions of the origin of the name barm brack: that it comes from the Irish bairgain breac – bread that is speckled; or that it derives from the use of barm, or yeast drawn off fermenting malt. Brack made at home, as often as not, is raised not with yeast but with baking powder and is called a tea brack because the dried fruit is soaked in tea. A barm brack, on the other hand, is raised with yeast (but not barm) and is bought from a bakery rather than baked at home. Both are eaten sliced and buttered.

Ingredients:

255 g/9 oz/1¼ US cups raisins

255 g/9 oz/1½ US cups sultanas

60 g/2 oz/scant ¼ US cup mixed (candied) peel (optional)

225 g/8 oz/1 generous US cup dark cane sugar

500 ml/16 fl oz/2 US cups Indian tea, hot, strong and black

350 g/12 oz/3 US cups (unsifted) plain white flour

2 teasp baking powder

1 teasp mixed spice

2 medium-sized eggs, beaten

a little honey for the glaze

a 20 cm/8 inch cake tin (at least 7.5 cm/3 inches deep) greased and lined with greaseproof (unwaxed) or non-stick paper

Method:

Place the fruit, sugar and peel in a bowl and pour the hot tea (without milk) over them; stir well until the sugar is dissolved, then stand overnight. Sift flour, baking powder and spice. Mix, alternately, some egg and some fruit into the flour, stirring thoroughly. When all the egg and fruit has been mixed in, add the ring and other charms if you are using them, making sure they are evenly distributed throughout the mix. For safety, wrap them in greaseproof paper.

Put the mixture in the cake tin and bake at 160°C/325°F/Gas 3 for about 1½ hours. About 10 minutes before it is ready, brush the top of the brack with warmed honey. Return to the oven until fully cooked. Cool in the tin for 15 minutes before turning out (glazed side up) on a rack.

ḣallowe'en puɗɗinɢ

This pudding is eaten at Hallowe'en in the Lower Ards area of Ulster. It could also make a lighter alternative to traditional Christmas pudding. 'Favours', which always including a ring — often a brass curtain ring — are placed in the pudding at Hallowe'en (for safety wrap this in greaseproof paper). The recipe was given to me by well-known food writer Honor Moore who hails from Newtownards and is a fund of knowledge on Ulster baking traditions.

SERVES 4–6

Ingredients:

60 g/2 oz/½ US cup unsifted white flour

90 g/3 oz butter, cut into small dice

110 g/4 oz/1 US cup wholemeal breadcrumbs

½ teasp bicarbonate of soda (baking soda)

1 teasp mixed spice

½ teasp salt

60 g/2 oz/¼ US cup caster sugar

225 g/8 oz/1¼ US cups mixed dried fruit

1 tablesp treacle

175 ml/6 fl oz/¾ US cup buttermilk

Method:

Sift the flour and place in a mixing bowl with the butter. Rub the butter into the flour until the mixture resembles breadcrumbs. Sift the soda, mixed spice and salt together and mix thoroughly into the flour mixture. Add all the other ingredients, using just enough buttermilk to give a soft but not sloppy mixture. Grease a 1 litre/2 lb/2 pint pudding bowl with butter (it should be large enough to allow the mixture to expand). Cover with a double thickness of greaseproof paper, making a pleat in the middle. Tie tightly with string, looping it across the centre to make a handle with which to lift the cooked pudding from the pot. Steam for about 3 hours.

Serve hot with whipped, fresh cream.

POTATO APPLE FARLS

A 'farl' is a triangular shape whose name (fardel) originally meant a fourth part of anything. This rough triangle cut from a circle is the traditional shape for potato cakes and griddle bread as well as for these rather unusual apple pastries. In some parts of the country they were served at Hallowe'en with the ring or 'favour' placed in just one cake. Originally they would have been cooked on a griddle over an open turf fire. They can be cooked on a heavy frying pan and can also be baked in a hot oven.

MAKES 4

Ingredients:

480 g/1 lb/4 US cups white flour

480 g/1 lb/3 generous US cups floury potatoes, mashed while hot

15 g/½ oz/1 tablesp butter, melted

½ teasp baking powder

4 large cooking apples (Bramley for preference) peeled, cored, and thinly sliced

honey or brown sugar, and butter, to taste

Method:

Mix the sifted flour and baking powder in a bowl; add the melted butter and the hot, mashed potatoes. Mix well, then knead lightly until you have a soft dough. Divide into two equal pieces.

Roll out the dough on a floured board until you have a circle 1cm/½ inch thick. Divide into four farls (triangles). Repeat with the other piece of dough. On each of four farls place an equal amount of the apple, then place another farl on top. Pinch the edges together to seal them well.

Cook over a medium heat on a griddle (or in a heavy frying pan) until brown on the bottom. Turn carefully and brown the other side. Now comes the tricky bit! Slit the pastries horizontally and lift off the tops. Add thin slices of butter and (depending how sweet you like your dessert) as much honey and/or sugar as you fancy. Carefully replace the tops and continue cooking for a few minutes until the butter and sugar have melted into a sauce. Serve hot.

Martinmas, 11 November

Folk tradition has it that this feast was established in gratitude to St Martin of Tours who is credited with conferring the monk's tonsure on St Patrick, whereupon Patrick killed a pig for every monk and nun in Ireland. In Celtic times it was traditionally one of the four days in the year when a pig was killed. This made agricultural sense; six to eight month-old pigs were also called 'the young pig of November', well-fattened on harvest gleanings and ready for slaughter and curing.

Widely celebrated until about a hundred years ago, this was a day associated with the ritual sacrifice of an animal to ensure good fortune. It was believed that bad luck came to anyone who failed to fulfil this custom. Strong farmers sacrificed a pig, a sheep, or lamb; more often it was just a fowl but it had to be the best bird in the flock or the charm did not work! To ensure that even the poorest could protect themselves it was customary for those who kept fowl, whether geese, ducks or hens, to make a gift of a fowl to poorer neighbours. Failing that, people bought live fowl at the local market so that they too could observe the Martinmas rite. As night fell on Martinmas Eve the woman of the house killed the bird. Its blood was then spilled over the threshold of the house, the bedpost, over the fireplace and in the cattle byre and outhouses. During the killing this prayer was spoken:

'I shed this blood in honour of God and St Martin to bring us safe from illness and disease in the coming year.'

The fowl was roasted and eaten on the feast day.

CONFIT OF DUCK LEG WITH ORANGE AND CARDAMOM JAM

A confit means a leg cooked in duck fat, very slowly (at 130°C) for about one and a half hours until tender and falling off the bone. The skin is crisped before serving. This dish was created by Derry Clarke of L'Ecrivain restaurant for the 2005 Irish Food Writers Guild annual Good Food Awards luncheon. Derry is one of Ireland's leading chefs. For a number of years now he has created recipes using Irish foods that have won Irish Food Writers Guild Food Awards. Silver Hill Ducks were award-winners in 2005 and their ready-cooked duck legs are widely available.

Serves 4

Ingredients:

4 Silver Hill ready-cooked (confit) duck legs

1–2 tablesp vegetable oil

250 ml/8 fl oz/1 cup fresh orange juice

125 g/4½ oz caster sugar

one half cinnamon stick

3 cardamom pods (opened and seeds removed)

2 oranges, peeled, segmented and chopped

Method:

Simmer juice, sugar and cinnamon in a heavy-based pan until reduced by half. Add the cardamom seeds and cook for a further 10 minutes. Cool. Place chopped orange pieces on kitchen paper to remove excess liquid. Add to the sauce, reheat briefly and serve with the duck.

Heat the oil in a pan wide enough to fit all four duck legs. Place the cooked duck legs, skin side down, in hot oil and cook until crisp and hot right through. Serve at once, accompanied by Celeriac and Potato Purée (next page).

celeriac and potato purée

Celeriac is a root vegetable with a high water content and makes for a softer, wetter purée than traditional champ dishes. Its knobbly appearance puts off many people, but the flavour, which is similar to celery, makes it an especially good accompaniment to game as well as to confit of duck (see recipe on previous page).

SERVES 4-6

Ingredients:

450 g/1 lb floury potatoes, peeled

900 g/2 lb celeriac (weighed after peeling)

60 g/2 oz butter

60 ml/2 fl oz/¼ cup cream

Method:

Steam the potatoes until tender. Dry, then put them through a potato ricer or mouli. Cut the celeriac into large chunks and boil in salted water until tender. Dry them off before puréeing in a food processor. Combine the two vegetables, then add butter and cream, season to taste, and mix well. Serve very hot.

Celeriac

The Twelve Days of Christmas

With the coming of Christianity in the fifth century the pagan midwinter festival held to mark the winter solstice was gradually replaced by Christmas. The twelve days run from Christmas Day, 25 December, to 6 January, the Feast of the Epiphany (Little Christmas) otherwise known as *Nollaig na mBan*, Women's Christmas.

This was and still is the biggest and longest festive season of the year. Preparations began well in advance. Christmas puddings and cakes are made in November to give these rich fruit and whisky-flavoured concoctions time to mature. In bygone days the season started with the 'big market', sometimes called the 'live market', because fowl to be eaten at Christmas were sold alive. A second market held shortly before Christmas was known as the 'dead market' where dead geese, turkeys and chickens were sold. Farmers travelled by pony and trap, even on foot, bringing with them the fowl, eggs, butter and vegetables they had produced. With the money earned, the women 'brought home the Christmas' – toys, clothes, dried fruit, spices and sugar for the cakes and puddings, and 'Christmas cheer' in the form of tobacco, whiskey, wine and the best China ale (as tea was called when it first arrived in Ireland).

It was common for the better off to send meat, butter, milk and eggs out to their workers, friends and poorer neighbours. It's a tradition that lives on in that, when doing the rounds of friends today, it's usual to bring a gift of festive or luxury food like a cake, chocolates or biscuits, as well as a bottle of cheer. Christmas Eve was observed as a fasting day in the past and the main meal was ling, cod, or hake served with parsley sauce and potatoes. The fast did not last until midnight, though. As soon as all the preparations for the next day were finished, the celebration would begin with the cutting of the cake and the drinking of tea and whiskey punch, with apples and sweets for the children.

Christmas dinner was, and still is, the most elaborate meal of the year. At home the appetiser is usually kept simple; perhaps a sliver of smoked salmon, or a wedge of melon, before the main course is served. In most homes roast stuffed goose would have been the festive bird and, although now an expensive luxury, it still remains so in some families.

Turkey is a less costly and popular choice, always accompanied by boiled or baked ham, a savoury stuffing, brussels sprouts, crisp roast potatoes and giblet gravy. It's a formidable meal and that's before the dessert arrives – a rich Christmas pudding with cream or a sherry trifle and, for those who still have room, mince pies.

The day after Christmas is the Christian feast of St Stephen, the first Christian martyr. In Irish folklore the wren was believed to have betrayed Stephen as he hid in the bushes from his enemies. That's why this poor inoffensive little bird was hunted by wren or 'wran' boys dressed up in fantastical costumes and paraded around by them on this day while they chanted:

'The wran, the wran, the King of all birds
On Stephen's day was caught in the furze:
Though his body was little his family was great,
So if it pleases your honour, give us a treat.'

The point was to collect money and food for a hooley. Although they don't actually hunt the wren any more, in many parts of the country wren boys still dress up and parade around, collecting money for charity.

Spiced beef was and is the traditional meat of Stephen's Day. This Irish delicacy can be eaten hot with a fruity sauce but, on St Stephen's Day, it is normally served cold, with simple accompaniments like a fruit-based chutney, wholemeal bread, pickled vegetables and salads.

New Year's Eve and New Year's Day have few traditions in the southern part of Ireland because 1 January was not the beginning of the (pagan) Irish new year – that was four weeks later in February. New Year is more widely celebrated in the North of Ireland, however, where there is a strong Scottish inheritance (the Scottish Hogmanay). But even in the South, church bells peal out at midnight, boats in harbours sound their fog horns, fireworks are set off and friends 'see the New Year in' at parties.

The twelfth day of Christmas, 6 January, the Feast of The Epiphany, was the day on which the Christmas tree was undressed and the household decorations taken down. Also known as *Nollaig na mBan*, Women's Christmas is still celebrated in rural areas, especially in the south and west, with a dainty feast of freshly baked scones with cream and preserves, with gingerbread, iced sponge cakes and tea (rather than strong drink).

chRISTMAS puddING

Christmas pudding was first served, as far as written accounts record, to William the Conqueror by his chef Robert Argyllion on the occasion of his coronation in 1066. No doubt it came to Ireland by way of our own Norman conquerors. It's a dish that has taken many twists and turns down the years: once it was a kind of meat stew; by Elizabethan times it had become a meat porridge sweetened with fruit; a century later it had solidified into the dark, rich pudding we know today.

MAKES 5 x 450 g/1lb puddings or about 20 individual puddings

Ingredients:

225 g/8 oz/2 US cups beef suet, weighed when shredded

225 g/8 oz/2 US cups self-raising flour, unsifted

225 g/8 oz/4 US cups fresh white breadcrumbs

225 g/8 oz/1¼ US cups stoned prunes, chopped finely

225 g/8 oz/1½ US cups currants

225 g/8 oz/1¼ US cups raisins

225 g/8 oz/1¼ US cups sultanas

225 g/8 oz/1 generous US cup soft, dark brown sugar

110 g/4 oz/½ US cup glacé (candied) cherries, washed and chopped

110 g/4 oz/½ US cup mixed (candied) peel, chopped

1 cooking apple, peeled and grated

1 carrot, peeled and grated

1 unwaxed lemon, grated zest and juice

1 unwaxed orange, grated zest and juice

6 medium-sized eggs, beaten

1 teasp mixed spice/allspice

½ teasp nutmeg, grated

½ teasp cinnamon, ground

1 teasp salt

300 ml/10 fl oz/1¼ US cups stout

Method:

Sift flour and spices together into a large mixing bowl. Mix in suet, breadcrumbs, dried fruits and sugar. Stir in the salt, peel, cherries, carrot and apple. Mix in eggs, stout, orange, lemon zest and juice. Fill mixture into bowls, leaving 5cm (2 inches) headspace for rising. Cover with two layers of greaseproof paper, leaving a pleat in the centre. Tie tightly, arranging a handle on the top for lifting from the pot. Top with foil. Place in a steamer or pot with the water coming halfway up the bowl. Steam for 6–7 hours, topping up with boiling water as needed.

For the individual, small puddings, place in a roasting tin (with water coming halfway up the containers), cover with a tent of tin foil, shiny side down, and steam in an oven set at 150°C/300°F/Gas 2 for 1½ hours.

To reheat: Cover with fresh paper and string. Steam a large pudding for 2–3 hours, individual ones for 1 hour.

Serve with plain, unsweetened whipped cream, or clotted cream.

Cook's Tip:

Unless you have a big family or a large number of guests for Christmas, there will be leftover pudding to deal with. In Dublin, wedges of pudding are fried gently in butter until hot through.

A more interesting approach is to take about 225 g/8 oz cold pudding, crumbed as fine as possible, and mix into a litre of slightly softened ice cream. Refreeze at once.

Christmas Pudding

MINCE PIES WITH IRISH WHISKEY

Mince pies were originally made with minced beef or lamb, mixed with spices and (when available) some fruit for flavouring. Over time the fruits became more important and the meat content was reduced. Nowadays the only element of meat in mincemeat is beef suet. It is hard to find ready-prepared suet but, given a little warning, any good, reputable craft butcher will provide you with a piece of fresh suet which can be easily grated with a coarse grater or chopped in a food processor. Although flaky (or puff) pastry was traditional for mince pies, it is very rich and high in fat; short crust pastry is more often used today.

MAKES about 2 x 450 g/1 lb jars mincemeat; 12 pies

Ingredients:

about 450 g/1 lb short crust pastry

For the mincemeat:

700 g/1 ½ lb/4 US cups dried fruit (equal proportions of sultanas, raisins and currants)

110 g/4 oz/¾ US cup mixed citrus peel (optional)

225 g/8 oz/a generous US cup moist dark-brown sugar (muscovado)

110 g/4 oz/1 US cup beef suet, shredded

60 g/2 oz/²/₃ US cup ground nuts (hazel or almonds)

1 large cooking apple, peeled, cored and finely chopped

1 teasp nutmeg, grated

½ teasp allspice, ground

½ teasp cinnamon, ground

1 lemon, zest and juice

125 ml/4 fl oz/½ US cup Irish whiskey

Method:

Make the filling two weeks in advance to allow the flavours to develop. In a large mixing bowl stir all the ingredients together until well mixed. Cover and leave in a cool place for 24 hours. Mix well again before potting into clean preserving jars. Cover tightly and store in a cool, dark place.

Lightly grease the base of a shallow 12-space bun tin. Roll out the pastry and use a 9 cm/3½ inch pastry cutter (or whatever size fits your bun tin) to cut out 24 rounds. Place one in each of the twelve bun tins then fill it with about a heaped teaspoon of the mincemeat. Dampen the edges of each pastry case before placing the remaining twelve pastries on top as lids. Press the edges together to seal firmly. Bake at 220°C/425°F/Gas 7 for about 20 minutes or until golden-brown. Remove the pies from the tin carefully and place them to cool on a wire rack. Dust with icing sugar.

Mince pies must be served warm. They are wonderful served with a little whipped cream.

spiced beef

Spices have been imported into Ireland since earliest times, but were always scarce and expensive, so this dish was one reserved for a festive feast, particularly at Christmas. It's a tradition that lives on today and no Christmas cold table is complete without it. Dry-spicing is the older, more interesting way of curing it, but it has to be said, wet spicing has its fans — some people even defend the modern butchers' method of 'spicing-up' corned beef which, although good to eat if you choose your butcher carefully, is not really the same at all. Do weigh the ingredients for this recipe carefully.

SERVES 6–10

Ingredients for Spicing:

about 2 kg/4½ lb beef (silverside, topside, round, rump, **or** brisket)

15 g/½ oz saltpetre

225 g/8 oz sea salt

30 g/1 oz allspice

30 g/1 oz whole black peppercorns

90 g/3 oz dark brown sugar

12 dried juniper berries (crushed)

a big pinch of ground cloves

2 bay leaves

Ingredients for Cooking:

bunch of thyme

bay leaves

1 onion, studded with cloves

1 carrot

1 stick celery

12 whole peppercorns

Method:

Mix the salt and saltpetre and rub some of it into the meat, making sure it gets well into all the hollows and cracks. Place in a glass or other non-metal bowl and keep covered in the fridge or another really cool place. Repeat this procedure every day for 4 days. Then grind the whole spices and mix them with the sugar, cloves and bay leaves. Rub this mixture into the beef and place in a clean dish. Store in the fridge. Every second day for 10–14 days, turn the joint over and rub in the spices that adhere to the meat.

To Cook:

Tie a bunch of thyme and a few bay leaves to the joint. Place it in a pot just large enough to fit the meat. Add an onion stuck with a few cloves, a carrot, a stick of celery and a dozen whole peppercorns. Cover with cold water (mixed, if you wish, with a bottle of stout, for a distinctive flavour). Bring to simmering point, cover tightly and cook in a low oven set to 140°C/275°F/ Gas 1 for about 5 hours. If you prefer, simmer it gently for about 3½ hours on the hob. It should be quite soft and tender when fully cooked.

Spiced beef can be eaten hot but it is more usual to serve it cold. To do this, allow it to cool in the cooking liquid for about 2 hours, then remove it, wrap in greaseproof paper, and press it lightly while stored in the fridge. Slice very thinly with a very sharp knife. It is often served as finger food on brown bread spread with a fruit chutney, with chopped pickles (sweet and sour pears, sweet pickled onions, or piccalilli are good), or as a plated dish with a green salad, or a celery and walnut salad, and crusty white bread and butter.

BUTTERMILK SCONES

Scones are the great standby of the Irish country kitchen. They can be made in a few minutes and eaten warm from the oven. With imagination, a plain scone can be transformed into a variety of sweet and savoury breads.

MAKES 8–12

Ingredients:

450 g/1 lb/4 US cups plain white flour

1 (scant) teasp bicarbonate of soda (bread/baking soda)

1 (scant) teasp baking powder

1 teasp salt

90 g/3 oz butter, cubed

1 egg, beaten (optional)

about 200 ml/7 fl oz/1 scant US cup buttermilk

Method:

Sift the flour, salt, bicarbonate of soda and baking powder together. Rub in the butter until the texture resembles breadcrumbs. Quickly and lightly mix in the egg and milk, using enough liquid to make a soft dough that is puffy and easy to roll out. Knead lightly – no more than six times. Roll out to 2–2½ cm/¾–1 inch thick (depending on how high and moist you prefer the finished scone). For even rising, cut out the scones with a fluted cutter dipped in flour, or with a very sharp knife. Transfer to a baking sheet with a palette knife. Bake immediately at 220°C/425°F/Gas 7 for 15–20 minutes, or until well risen and brown.

Variations:

Savoury: Use half plain white and half fine-ground wholemeal flour.
Add 175 g/6 oz/1¼ US cups grated hard cheese (extra mature Cheddar, or Gabriel from the West Cork Cheese Company), or Parmesan.
Brush with milk and sprinkle about 2 tablesp of poppy seeds over the top.

Sweet: Mix in 1 tablespoon of sugar and 3 or 4 tablespoons of sultanas.
Mix in 1–2 finely chopped dessert apples (peeled and cored) and a teaspoon of ground nutmeg (or cinnamon) or add about six dried apricots, finely chopped.

Weddings and Christenings

Marriages were of great importance, especially in rural Ireland where it was considered a neglect of social duty not to marry; spinsters and bachelors had a lower status than married men and women.

Neighbours, relatives and friends were invited to the house of the bride for feasting, music, singing and dancing into the wee small hours. On the return journey from the church to the wedding party the groom was often halted by small boys holding a rope across the road; he could buy his passage with a small gift of money. When the bride arrived home her mother broke a small piece of 'bride cake' over her head.

This bride, or wedding, cake was often no more than a wheat cake flavoured with honey and fruit. Breaking the cake over the head of the bride brought good fortune and prosperity to the couple and then, by sharing out the cake among the guests, their guests shared in 'the luck'. Today, the bridal couple, both holding the knife, make the first cut in the cake, which is then divided and distributed to the guests. Small pieces of the cake are packed into little cardboard boxes and sent to members of the family and friends who have not been able to attend the wedding. Over time the cake developed from a wheat cake into a rich fruit cake, covered with a thick layer of marzipan, then iced with highly decorated Royal (hard) icing. Although many modern couples are now opting for madeira, lemon, chocolate and other varieties of lighter cake as an alternative, the rich fruit cake is still very popular at Irish weddings. There can be as many as three or four tiers on the cake.

After the marriage ceremony, guests attend a wedding reception, which is usually held in a hotel but sometimes in the home of the bride. The wedding 'feast' is a formal luncheon or dinner which ends with the cutting of the wedding cake, speeches, and a champagne toast to the couple. Additional guests may arrive for an evening of entertainment.

Christening is a religious ceremony at which a newborn baby is baptised and made a member of its parents' church and given a Christian name. The parents invite relatives and close friends to attend the ceremony and afterwards to gather for a small, informal party. One of the tiers of the parents' wedding cake may have been preserved to be served and those present will 'wet the baby's head' with a drink.

MUSSELS BAKED WITH SEA SPINACH & ST TOLA ORGANIC GOATS CHEESE

Otto and Hilde Kunze run a restaurant in Dunworly, County Cork. Both are totally committed to the organic philosophy and a meal at Otto's Creative Catering is an experience no visitor to West Cork should miss. They grow a stunning range of vegetables and fruit. They bake bread, cure and smoke a variety of meats and seafoods and make good use of the wild harvest of the Atlantic shore which is just yards away. Otto writes: 'At a beach near you, the winter storms throw seaweed beyond the high tide mark and this thick mat of composting material is the best growing medium for the sea-spinach (which looks very similar to the cultivated) but has thicker leaves shining in a stronger, brighter green. It can be harvested virtually all year round, except when it goes to seed (May to September) because the taste goes a bit too strong. Pick just the young leaves (no stems) and wash carefully in cold water to remove any sand. If you can't get the wild spinach go for the next best, the organically grown.'

Ingredients:

3 kg/7 lb mussels

1 large onion, peeled, chopped finely

50 g/1½ oz butter

3 cloves garlic, peeled and crushed

1 teasp black pepper

300 ml/10 fl oz/1¼ US cup dry white wine

3 kg sea spinach

255 g/9 oz St Tola organic goats cheese

For the sauce:

50 g/1½ oz butter

50 g/1½ oz flour

150 ml/5 fl oz/²⁄₃ US cup of the cooking juices from the mussels

150 ml/5 fl oz/²⁄₃ US cup dry white wine

150 ml/5 fl oz/²⁄₃ US cup cream ground nutmeg, salt, pepper and lemon juice to taste

SERVES 4 as a main course; 8–10 as a starter

Method:

Choose mussels carefully; the shells should be either tightly closed or, when given a sharp tap, should close promptly. Scrub shells thoroughly with a hard brush and remove the beards (the tuft of fibres projecting from the shell). Chop the onion and fry in the butter until golden. Add the garlic, black pepper, wine and mussels. Cover with a tight-fitting lid and bring to the boil. Toss the mussels a few times (with the lid on) and cook for about 5 minutes. Discard any that have not opened. Remove mussels from the pot; strain the cooking liquid and reserve for the sauce. Pick the mussels out of the shells.

Blanch the spinach in boiling water for 2 minutes; drain and refresh in cold water. Strain, squeezing out all the water, and chop coarsely.

Melt the butter in a pot, add the flour and cook for a few minutes. Add equal quantities of wine, cream and strained mussel cooking juice. Bring slowly to the boil, whisking all the time and adding more mussel juice until the sauce has a good creamy consistency. Taste and season quite strongly with the salt, pepper, nutmeg and lemon juice so that the spinach will be well flavoured.

Add spinach to the sauce, warm. Place in a big Pyrex dish and add the mussels; crumble the soft fresh goats cheese on top and bake at 220°C/425°F/Gas 7 for 15 minutes (or until the cheese is slightly browned).

You may also divide and bake the mixture in 8–10 small ramekins.

BEEF FILLET BAKED IN A TURF CRUST

This comes from Evan Doyle in The Strawberry Tree restaurant at the Brooklodge Hotel, Macreddin Village, near Aughrim, County Wicklow. Evan writes of this unusal recipe: 'This is a recipe that we have the opportunity to use both for large functions like weddings and also for smaller numbers in the restaurant. It's a very, very simple recipe that's based on salt crust baking, but uses peat moss [milled turf] instead and to the same end effect – the moisture of the meat being trapped inside by the turf produces a really moist and juicy dish on the inside enhanced by an earthy, Irishy 'terroir' flavour on the outside. For a small amount of beef, as in a fillet for 2 or 4 people, a 1 kg/2lb loaf tin can be used or, for larger cuts like half a strip sirloin, a large deep baking dish is perfect. As in salt crusting, line the base with an inch of turf, place the meat on top and then completely cover with more turf and press firm. Sprinkle with a small amount of water and cover with fork-pricked tin foil.' The following recipe is for a large party.

Ingredients:

I striploin, or fillet, of organic beef

I bag of peat moss

salt, black pepper

Method:

Season the beef very well with the salt and pepper, rubbing in all over. Line the base of a deep baking dish with a layer of peat moss, place the meat into the tin and cover completely with more peat, pressing it until it is firm. Put into a pre-heated oven at 160°C/325°F/Gas 3 and cook for 1½ to 2 hours depending on size. Because you cannot make visual checks or test with a skewer it's essential to use a meat probe to test the internal temperature of the meat at the centre of the joint. A temperature of 50°C will give you rare meat. Break the crust, lift out the meat and use kitchen paper to remove the attached turf, leaving just a fine, fine covering for taste. Let it rest for 15–20 minutes, then slice and serve.

PEPPER-CRUSTED LOIN OF VENISON

WITH SAUTÉED TURNIP AND POTATO, AND WHISKEY AND SHALLOT JUS

This recipe comes from John Luke, Head Chef at Rathsallagh Country House in Dunlavin, County Wicklow. Kay and Joe O'Flynn run this large rambling house in an idyllic low-key style. Great food, warm hospitality and surroundings that are quiet or romantic, to suit the day, make this an ideal venue for small weddings.

SERVES 4

Ingredients:

800 g/1¾ lb loin of venison, cut into 4 equal pieces

For the marinade:

300 ml/10 fl oz/1¼ US cups olive oil

zest of one orange and one lemon

3 shallots, sliced

2 cloves garlic, crushed

3 sprigs thyme

3 bay leaves

12 whole peppercorns

8 juniper berries, toasted

For the venison:

110 g/4 oz mixed peppercorns, crushed

2 tablesp olive oil

60 g/2 oz butter

500 ml/16 fl oz/2 US cups Irish whiskey

500 ml/16 fl oz/2 US cups chicken stock

10 shallots finely chopped

200 g/7 oz butter or crème frâiche

For the sautéed potato and swede turnip:

450 g/1 lb swede turnip, cut into julienne (the thickness of a matchstick)

200 g/7 oz potato, cut into julienne

4 tablesp oil

60 g/2 oz butter

Method:

Place venison steaks into marinade and refrigerate for 12 to 24 hours.

Crush peppercorns roughly (take a heavy skillet pan and use it as a mortar if you don't own a mortar and pestle). Take out the venison from the marinade and pat dry with kitchen paper. Season with salt and roll each steak through the crushed peppercorns.

Heat a heavy skillet pan over medium-high heat, add 2 tablespoons of oil and sear venison on both sides for 1–1½ minutes until nicely brown. Add 60g/2 oz butter at room temperature and turn down heat. Cook both sides for approximately 3 minutes a side, basting occasionally. Set aside venison to allow time for it to rest.

To make the whiskey and shallot sauce, pour fat from your skillet pan and add the finely chopped shallots, sweat briefly until they are translucent, take pan from heat and add whiskey; return to the heat to flame and reduce by half (be careful – the whiskey is liable to flambé). Add chicken stock and cook until reduced by half. Add 150g/5 oz of butter or crème frâiche to thicken the sauce.

While the sauce is cooking, heat a frying pan over high heat. Add 4 tablesp oil and 60g/2 oz butter. Sauté the julienne potatoes until they start to turn golden-brown, add the julienne turnip and continue to cook over medium-high heat for about 2 minutes. Add a tiny bit of water or chicken stock if the turnip begins to burn and turn down the heat slightly. Season with salt and pepper to taste.

Assembly:

Pack turnip and potato tightly into a ring mould and place in the centre of plate.

turnip

After allowing the venison to rest for 7–10 minutes, reheat it quickly for 4 minutes in an oven set at 250°C/475°F/Gas 9. Slice each venison steak into 6 pieces cut at a slight bias against the grain of the meat. Fan the venison on top of the vegetables and ladle sauce around plate and over the meat.

a whiskey cream dessert

Irish Mist was the first widely marketed Irish liqueur and is based upon a long-lost recipe from the past. The story goes that an Austrian refugee ended up in Tullamore town, long a bastion of Irish whiskey distilling, clutching 'an old Irish recipe' that had been in his family for a very long time. Irish Mist is based on that recipe. True or not, the result is a very distinctive liqueur.

SERVES 4

Ingredients:

90 g/3 oz butter

60 g/2 oz flour

375 ml/12 fl oz/1½ US cups milk

60 g/2 oz caster sugar

4 large eggs (separated)

2 tablesp Irish Mist liqueur

Method:

Beat the egg whites until stiff, adding the sugar, as if you were making meringues. Make a roux with the butter and flour, stirring over a gentle heat for 2 minutes. Add in the milk and stir to mix it through. Cook gently for 5 minutes. Add the Irish Mist liqueur. Allow to cool slightly, then beat in the egg yolks, one at a time. Stir in one tablespoon of the stiffly beaten egg whites, then fold in the remainder. Turn out gently into a two-pint soufflé dish. Bake at once for 40–45 minutes in a preheated oven at 190°C/375°F/Gas 5. Serve with a sauce of raspberries, blackberries or fraughans (wild blueberries).

Fruit Sauce:

The raspberries will need no sweetening. Just pass the fruit through a mouli-sieve to remove the seeds. Blackberries and fraughans will need roughly 1lb of sugar for each 1lb of fruit. Simply stew the fruit and the sugar together, gently, until the sugar has completely dissolved and the fruit is soft; then work the mixture through the mouli-sieve to remove the skins and seeds. These sauces can all be prepared in advance and re-heated to serve with the soufflé.

IRISH WHISKEY-FED WEDDING/CHRISTENING CAKE

Feeding this traditional rich fruit cake with whiskey keeps it moist and allows the cake to be made well in advance of the celebration. For best results choose high quality dried fruit, sulphur-free, if possible. Although many people are skilled in the craft of decorative icing, this task is often left to professionals.

Ingredients:

450 g/1 lb/3 US cups currants

175 g/6 oz/1 US cup sultanas

175 g/6 oz/1 scant US cup raisins

60 g/2 oz/¹/₃ US cup glacé cherries, washed and chopped

60 g/2 oz/¹/₃ US cup mixed citrus peel, finely chopped

225 g/8 oz/2 US cups unsifted plain white flour

1 teasp ground cinnamon

1 teasp ground nutmeg

1 teasp ground dry ginger

60 g/2 oz/scant ½ US cup chopped almonds

225 g/8 oz/1 generous US cup dark brown sugar

1 tablesp treacle, warmed

225 g/8 oz unsalted butter

3 large eggs

grated zest of 1 unwaxed lemon

grated zest of 1 unwaxed orange

3 tablesp Irish whiskey, and more to feed the cake

For the Marzipan:

225 g/ 8 oz/2½ US cups ground almonds

110 g/4 oz/ 1US cup icing sugar

110 g/4 oz/ 1US cup caster sugar

1 teasp lemon juice

1 medium-sized egg, beaten

For the Royal Icing:

2 egg whites

450 g/1 lb/4 US cups icing sugar

1 teasp lemon juice

1 teasp glycerine

Method:

The night before baking take all the dried fruit and sprinkle it with the whiskey; cover and leave to absorb the flavour.

Grease a 20cm/8 inch round (or an 18cm/7 inch square) loose-based,deep cake tin and line with greaseproof paper. Sift the flour and spices together into a bowl. Cream the butter and sugar together until very light, pale and fluffy. Beat one tablespoon of flour into the creamed butter and sugar, then beat in the eggs, one tablespoon at a time. Do this very thoroughly and, if the mixture appears to be splitting or curdling, add a little flour before the next addition of egg. Fold in the flour. Now stir in all the remaining ingredients. You will have a stiff mixture by now – if it seems too stiff add a little cider. Place the mixture in the cake tin, spreading it out and making a depression in the centre (gently) with the back of a spoon.

It is traditional to tie a band of brown paper around the tin (to prevent scorching) but few people bother. However, you should have a double thickness sheet of greaseproof paper at the ready to place on the top of the cake if the top is becoming too browned. Bake at 130°C/275°F/Gas 1 on a shelf below the middle of the oven for 4¼–4¾ hours. Do not on any account open the door of the oven in the early stages. After about 3 hours it is safe to check it at odd intervals and cover the top if it seems necessary. But close the oven door gently! The cake is done when you cannot hear a trace of a sizzling sound and a skewer inserted into the centre come out clean. Cool in the tin.

Turn out, remove the paper, and wrap in a double thickness of fresh paper and store in a tin to mature for 6–8 weeks. Feed at intervals with Irish whiskey by making several holes in the top with a thin skewer or darning needle and dribbling in teaspoons of whiskey. Allow it to soak in, then re-wrap. At the next feeding time, do the bottom; and then do the sides.

A few days before the event, glaze the cake (top, or top and sides if both are being iced) with 2 tablesp redcurrant jelly melted in an equal amount of water. Cover with marzipan/almond paste (method p25) and allow to dry well before spreading the royal icing smoothly over the cake using a palette knife. Icing: Whisk eggs whites until frothy. Stir in half the sugar until dissolved. Whisk in rest of sugar, a little at a time. Add lemon juice and glycerine and whisk until the icing is light, fluffy and forms peaks. Dry for 24 hours before decorating.

Wakıng The Dead

A wake is a significant social occasion in the Irish tradition and is every bit as much about celebrating the life of the dead person as mourning their death. A wake is the period when friends and neighbours, often travelling long distances, gather in the house of the dead to pay their respects to the corpse , which used to be laid out in the best room.

When they arrive they go into the room to say a prayer, sympathise with the close relatives and then, duty done, settle down to enjoy themselves with the other mourners. They tell stories about the deceased and exchange gossip.

In bygone days traditional wake games like forfeits and spin-the-bottle were played. Courtships might be started and, sometimes, marriages arranged. Snuff and clay pipes were handed around to the older men and women and copious amounts of food and drink were provided for all. Neighbours helped with preparing the traditional foods: baked funeral meats, great loaves of bread, sometimes a special cake, and always ample amounts of *poitín*, beer, port wine, whiskey and tea. Amongst the poor of Dublin, coddle (always known as Dublin Coddle) was a less costly alternative to joints of ham and beef.

That waking the dead still exists in modern Ireland is shown by contemporary death notices in the newspapers which, if the family don't want people to call, contain the words 'house private'. Although all-night wakes are a thing of the past, people do usually call to the house to sympathise with the relatives. After the funeral, relatives and close friends are invited either to a local hotel for a light lunch, or 'back to the house' where, in rural areas, it's the practice for neighbours and friends to help prepare a meal of cooked meats and salads.

The custom of the 'American wake' took root after the Great Famine when emigration was at its peak. Friends and neighbours gathered in the house the night before an emigrant left. The party often went on all night and when the time came to go, friends would convey the emigrant part of the way along the road. In those days the journey was long and dangerous and parents said goodbye to their young sons and daughters knowing they might not meet again; the parting was, in essence, a death farewell.

BAKED HAM WITH CIDER, MUSTARD & APPLE SAUCE

Baked ham remains one of the traditional 'funeral meats' for wakes. Whole ham weighs 8–11 lbs and serves 14–16 people. A half ham from the fillet end weighs 4–5½ lbs and serves 6–10. A ham from the hock end contains more bone and serves 4–8 max.

Ingredients:

joint of ham

onion, peeled

carrot

celery stalk

bay leaf

8 whole black peppercorns

For the glaze:

1–2 whole cloves

250 ml/8 fl oz/1 US cup freshly squeezed orange juice

2–3 tablesp Demerara sugar

1 teasp mustard powder

For the sauce:

Bramley cooking apple, peeled, cored and chopped

300 ml/10 fl oz cider

1 teasp sugar, or to taste

1 tablesp wholegrain Irish mustard

2 teasp butter

Method:

Soak joint for 12 hours in two changes of water. Place in a large pot, add vegetables, bay leaf and peppercorns and cover with cold water. Bring slowly to simmering point, cover and barely simmer for 25 minutes for each 450 g/1 lb (for joints over 3.5 kg/8 lb, allow 20 minutes per 450 g/1 lb). Leave to cool a little in its cooking liquid off the heat. Lift out and remove the skin, leaving the fat. Mix sugar and dry mustard powder and press evenly all over the joint. With a sharp knife cut a lattice pattern in the fat. Press back any coating that falls off. Stick a clove into the cuts where the lines cross. Heat oven to 220°C/425°F/Gas 7. Place the ham in a roasting tin surrounded by the orange juice. Bake for about 20 minutes or until the sugar has slightly caramelised.

Cook the apple in the cider and sugar until soft. Beat with a wooden spoon until smooth. Stir in the mustard and butter and season to taste.

Baked ham is often served cold with a variety of salads.

ÐUBLIN COÐÐLE

Said to have been a favourite dish of Jonathan Swift, Dean of St Patrick's Cathedral and author of the famous Gulliver's Travels, this dish is now rarely eaten outside Dublin. In the area of the inner city known as the Liberties it is a favourite Saturday night dish as well as a funeral food. The reason is purely practical – it doesn't spoil if left cooking for an extra hour or two.

SERVES 4–6

Ingredients:

450 g/1 lb bacon bits*, **or** a streaky bacon joint, cubed

450 g/1 lb good quality (meaty) Irish breakfast sausages

3 large onions, peeled, and chopped

1 ¼ kg/3 lb floury potatoes, peeled

6 tablesp fresh parsley, chopped

freshly ground black pepper to taste

500 ml/16 fl oz/2 cups water

*Bacon 'bits' are off-cuts from various types of bacon (both smoked and pale) and are sold cheaply in Dublin pork butchers' shops specially for coddle. Normally they contain a fairly even mixture of fat and lean. Streaky bacon also works well; keep the skin on for more flavour.

Method:

Cut the potatoes into fairly large pieces (leave them whole if small). Chop the fresh parsley. Choose a heavy pot with a really tight-fitting lid. Put a generous layer of chopped onions on the bottom and then layer the other ingredients, giving each layer a generous twist of pepper. Bring to the boil, then reduce the heat to a bare simmer. Cover very tightly. Cook for 2–5 hours! The longer and slower the cooking, the better this dish will be. It cannot come to any harm providing the lid is really tight. A very low oven is best, set at 120°C/250°F/Gas ½.

In some homes, what my son once christened 'slithery' (boiled and not browned) sausages are disliked. You can either lay all the sausages on top and, just before serving, set the pot under a grill to brown them. Or, even better, remove the sausages to brown under a hot grill just before serving, although this will probably be anathema to the coddle purists!

Dublin Coddle is traditionally served with buttered white soda bread and bottles of stout. You can also serve it with quickly-cooked green cabbage.

wbite soda bread

In most parts of Ireland this bread is shaped and baked just like brown soda bread. However, in Ulster it is called a soda 'farl' and, rather than a round loaf, it is usually rolled out into a flat, round cake about 2 cm/ ¾ inch thick, then scored on both sides into 4 even sections called farls. It is then lightly dusted with flour and cooked slowly (turned once) on a griddle or a heavy frying pan until cooked through and light brown.

Ingredients:

625 g/1 lb 6 oz/5¼ US cups plain white flour

1 teasp (generous) bicarbonate of soda

1 teasp salt

About 450 ml/15 fl oz/(scant) 2 US cups buttermilk

Method:

Preheat the oven to 200°C/400°F/Gas 6. Mix the flour, salt and soda in a mixing bowl. Add only enough buttermilk to make a soft dough. Flour your hands and the work surface and knead lightly by hand until the dough is smooth. Shape into a circle about 4 cm/1½ inches deep. Take a sharp, well-floured knife and cut a deep cross in the top. Place on a baking sheet and bake for 40–45 minutes. To see if it is fully cooked, test by tapping the bottom and listening for a hollow sound. Cool on a wire rack, or, if you like a soft crust, wrapped in a linen or cotton tea-cloth. Eat the same day.